This loving, nostalgic memoir of a  1955–1965, weaves personal with happenings in her family to her national and international events. The family-kampong events include the coming of TV to Potong Pasir, the national includes Lee Kuan Yew campaigning there and the international impact of the news of the assassination of President Kennedy. In this way, the author imbues the seemingly small things with social significance, fusing drama, comedy and tragedy into a poignant tale of a child growing up. In addition, as she matures, she becomes aware of her Peranakan and feminist heritages, and how her mother empowered her by sending her to an English school. If you want to know what it was like for Singapore to progress exponentially from the third to the first world, this book is an essential document. It is an invaluable companion to her earlier book *Frog Under a Coconut Shell*.

Robert Yeo,
Author of ONE – The Anthology, *poet, playwright and novelist*

This book gives a fascinating insight into life in a Singaporean Kampong during the transition from British rule to self-government with comparisons at different levels of living conditions. Josephine's remarkable recall of childhood memories is fascinating ... This is a very well written book with vivid descriptions that are believable. It could be a useful reference book for students of the history of Singapore.

Jennie Lisney,
Vice President of UK's Society of Woman Writers & Journalists

"The story of Singapore needs to be a key part of the psyche
of every citizen which motivates him (or her)
to excel and bonds him (or her) to Singapore."

Mr Goh Chok Tong
Prime Minister 1990 to 2004
Straits Times, *22nd July 1996*

KAMPONG SPIRIT
Gotong Royong

Life in Potong Pasir, 1955 to 1965

To
William
A gift from Mame Dad,
with best wishes,

Josephine Chia Josephine Chia
— March 2015

PS
Hope this brings back good memories
of your kampong days!

Marshall Cavendish
Editions

Front cover: Bernard Go Kwang Meng

Published 2013
Marshall Cavendish Editions
An imprint of Marshall Cavendish International
1 New Industrial Road, Singapore 536196

Other Marshall Cavendish Offices
Marshall Cavendish Corporation. 99 White Plains Road, Tarrytown NY 10591-9001,
USA • Marshall Cavendish International (Thailand) Co Ltd. 253 Asoke,
12th Floor, Sukhumvit 21 Road, Klongtoey Nua, Wattana, Bangkok 10110, Thailand
• Marshall Cavendish (Malaysia) Sdn Bhd, Times Subang, Lot 46, Subang Hi-Tech
Industrial Park, Batu Tiga, 40000 Shah Alam, Selangor Darul Ehsan, Malaysia.

Marshall Cavendish is a trademark of Times Publishing Limited

National Library Board, Singapore Cataloguing-in-Publication Data
Chia, Josephine.
Kampong spirit gotong royong : life in Potong Paisr, 1955 to 1965 / Josephine Chia.
– Singapore : Marshall Cavendish Editions, 2013.
p. cm.
ISBN : 978-981-4398-60-2 (pbk.)

1. Communities – Singapore – Social life and customs. 3. Lifestyles – Singapore.
I. Title.

HN655.2.C6
307.095957 – dc23   OCN823784086

Printed in Singapore by Markono Print Media Pte Ltd

This book is dedicated to my grandchildren
Jeremiah, Emmanuel, Amelia and Mattheus,
and to all the children of Singapore
who hold the future of our nation in their hands.

Contents

Acknowledgements

I WISH TO thank National Arts Council (NAC) for their generous Arts Creation Fund which made it possible for me to concentrate on writing this book. I am also grateful to the NAC for giving the publishing grant to Marshall Cavendish to publish this book.

I would also like to thank the National Archives for permission to use some of their photographs. Photo credits and thanks also go to Mr Lim Kheng Chye and Mr Han Chou Yuan.

The first incarnation of *Balik Kampong* was published in the *Peranakan* magazine, by the Peranakan Association; and its second incarnation was subsequently published in National Library Board's *Singapore Memories* archives.

I wish to also acknowledge the use of a couple of books which helped to refresh my memory and confirm some of the facts. These are:

- *Singapore – An Illustrated History, 1941–1984,* Text and Edited by Daljit Singh & VT Arasu. Published by the Information Division, Ministry of Culture.
- *Chronicle Of Singapore, 1959–2009,* Edited by Peter HL Lim. Published by EDM and NLB.

- Non-specific Articles from NLB Singapore Infopedia, newspaper articles and from the National Archives.
- The quotation by Mr Goh Chok Tong is taken from *Our place in Time – Exploring Heritage And Memory in Singapore*, edited by Kwok Kim Woon et al. Published by Singapore Heritage Society,1996.
- The lyrics of P. Ramlee's song 'Getaran Jiwa' is taken from the film, *Anatara Dua Drajat* by the Shaw Brothers. Its English translation was gleaned from various translations on the web.

I have been lucky to get two excellent editors for this book. Jennie Lisney, United Kingdom, came in when the manuscript was still under the NAC Arts Creation Fund Process. Tara Hasnain was appointed when Marshall Cavendish accepted the manuscript. I am amazed what good editors can pick up when the writer herself is blinded by her own words. So thank you both!

Foreword

EVERYONE WANTS TO be happy. Only the degree differs. How avidly one wants to pursue this happiness depends on how much it matters to the individual. This quest starts from satisfying the basic needs of having a home, nourishment, good health and family. Yet somehow it morphs into an obsession to possess more and more things, as if somehow material acquisitions can satisfy the inner longing of the spirit.

Modern Singapore has all the trappings of material success.

This is not something to belittle, as it has taken hard work, dedication and good leadership, for our country to transform itself from a swamp-infested island, where many people lived below the breadline, to a striving metropolis where the majority of the population are in comfortable housing and living well. And yet there is a growing sense that this never-ending race to acquire all the material comforts isn't giving us true happiness. People are beginning to look at other worthwhile pursuits that would satisfy the deep yearnings within their psyche.

It surprised many modern Singaporeans to discover that the Singapore folk, particularly those who had lived in our now-vanished kampongs with their lack of material comforts, of proper sanitation, of running water in the houses, of electricity and even food, had still seemed rather happy with that life. What was the quintessential quality that these rural people had, which had helped them get through their challenging lives with smiles on their faces and gratitude in their hearts?

It was the 'Kampong Spirit': *Gotong Royong.*

Gotong Royong is a Malay word which describes the coming together of the community to help and sustain each other. Multi-racial communities lived in the kampong like an extended family where everyone's doors were kept open, neighbours kept a look-out for each other, and the children played with one another without any thought of discriminating against the others for being of a different race. This is kampong spirit at its best.

Everyone needs someone. When the kampong spirit is in evidence, nobody needs to feel alone or abandoned. This warm feeling of being cared for makes life meaningful and brings happiness. And being happy, one possesses a stronger foundation, better able to take the knocks of life more easily.

The stories in this book show how the villagers of Kampong Potong Pasir coped with their deprivations and their challenges. Though having little, their joy was expressed because they lived together in a real community, in the spirit of sharing.

Each story has its own title and can stand alone without reference to the others, except for the first story, *Balik Kampong,* which acts as a kind of introduction and a general umbrella for all the other stories. The second story begins in 1955 and then the stories move progressively through the years till 1965.

This book will evoke memories of old Singapore for those of you who have lived through it. For the young, these stories will provide you with a view of the foundation your heritage is based on, and show you how far Singapore has come from its colonial days, and therefore you can be proud to celebrate your belonging to this marvellous nation.

Happy reading!

Josephine

Balik Kampong

FOOD CONSTITUTES A major part of the average Peranakan's life, whether it is cooking, eating or talking about it. It certainly is in mine! It is interesting how the memory or smell of a particular dish can evoke a strong response. Especially for a foodie like me. (Or you can say *piggy*!) The availability or lack of a particular food in one's childhood can be deeply ingrained in one's memories. And so it is with me.

I am amazed at how the memory of the smell of a specific food can pull me back to my childhood in *Kampong Potong Pasir*. Even though it might be snowing heavily outside my window in England and I am tucked up warm under a goose-down duvet in the twenty-first century, I can be resurrected again into my family's attap hut in 1950s Singapore. A *kampong* is a Malay word for *village*. The Malays were, after all, the indigenous people of Singapore.

What a delight it was to be awakened by the delicious fragrance of coconut milk boiling with the rice to be made into *nasi lemak*, my mother's pièce de résistance. The fragrance flooded our little attap-hut. Memories of food and my childhood are invariably linked with intimate memories of my mother, whom we called *Mak*. If we were lucky, we would get to eat the *nasi lemak*. At other times, Mak would scoop the cooked coconut rice, add the *sambal*, *ikan bilis* and various condiments and place them on banana leaves, wrapping them into green pyramids. She put them all in a rattan basket and my eldest brother, in his draw-string shorts, was the first in the family to cart them round the *kampong*, calling out, "*Nasi Lemak! Nasi Lemak! Lima Sen!* Coconut Rice! Coconut Rice! Five cents!"

The kampong, located off Upper Serangoon Road, was down the hill from Woodsville, which we called *Atas Bukit*. Near our village was a Christian cemetery called *Bidadari* which was allegedly named after a Malay fairy. It was the best known and most well-kept cemetery on our island. Unlike the slightly ominous atmosphere of the Chinese and Malay cemeteries, the Christian cemetery had a look of peace and serenity with its neat rows of graves, its tidy lawn and white marble tomb-stones. Entered through either of the sets of giant Victorian wrought-iron gates, the cemetery sprawled over a few acres of land. With its undulating topography of green fields and trees, it conveyed a hint of the rolling hills of the South Downs of England, so perhaps that was why the British chose the area as the last resting place for their dead.

Our village was predominantly Malay, and it suited us Peranakans, since we spoke more Malay than Chinese. Mak is the short form of the Malay word, *emak*, or *mother*. Our family managed with a bit of Teochew and Hokkien, but not Mandarin. As our Peranakan ancestry is from the Malacca line as opposed to the Penang line, we spoke the *Baba* patois, a rich hybrid of Malay and Hokkien; with an occasional mangled English, Dutch or Portuguese word. My mother wore the *sarong-kebaya* all her life, a Malay costume which Peranakans incorporated as our own. She always looked elegant and feminine in it. At home, my father, whom we called Ah Tetia, wore a singlet with the male sarong, usually patterned in stripes or checks rather than the floral batik of the female sarongs.

Like many Peranakan women in the old days, my mother was a skilled seamstress and an excellent cook. At one time she had servants to order about in the kitchen in my grandparents' magnificent house in Malacca in the Federated States of Malaya,

"Chop this! *Gilling* that! *Tumbok belachan!*"

I can imagine her with her arms akimbo or outstretched, pointing to this and that. She was never an aggressive person, her face was sweet and demure but she learnt from her mother that a household had to be run properly, and therefore servants had to be directed to perform well. However, subsequently the family fell upon bad times and she ended up in the shanty village of Potong Pasir with my father.

"Whatever your circumstances, always live with joy," Mak used to say.

She was always optimistic, and often sprouted philosophical sayings like those which intrigued me. After all, she was uneducated. Where was the wisdom coming from? It was the trigger which made me want to find out more about her.

Our kampong was within walking distance of Sennett Estate and the fabled *Alkaff Gardens*. The gardens were splendidly laid out alongside part of the sprawling Bidadari cemetery. Shaik Alkaff was a Yemeni from the Alkaff family, who came over from

Indonesia in 1852. He loved old Japan, so styled the gardens like a Japanese tea garden with a restaurant, tea kiosks, artificial lake and a replica of Mount Fuji. The spot was a popular recreational place and was so scenic that many of the Shaw Brothers' films were shot there – Singapore's first home-grown films, with our own home-grown actors. The most well-known and talented of them all was the dashing Malay actor, musician and director, P. Ramlee. He was handsome, had a pencil-thin moustache and a charismatic smile. And I had an adolescent crush on him.

"Ah Phine," he would say in my dreams. "I'm so in love with you! Please marry me!"

I don't know why Chinese villagers were fond of adding the '*Ah*' as prefix to a name. They also liked naming people by their characteristic, *Ah Sang* (Hokkien for someone who was thin), *Ah Puii* (for someone who was fat). Malays would say *Chichak Kurus* (Thin Lizard), or *Si Gemok* (That Fat Person). Nobody took offence or mentioned the discrimination act!

Nobody called me Josephine. The three syllable foreign name was a mouthful for the majority of the kampong folk who were not English educated or literate. Peranakans tended to be Buddhists or Taoists. But my family was converted to Catholicism by English missionaries who gave us food, clothing – and new names. Converts like us were called 'rice-bowl Christians' – people who converted not because we believed that a Christian God will save us from hell-fire but because we were hungry.

When I was a teenager, I slept on a mattress on the floor of our attap-hut. There were only two beds in our home, placed head to foot against each other. One was for my father who slept with two of my brothers; the other was for my mother who slept with two younger sisters. My baby brother slept in a sarong-cradle. I was made to sleep next to my third elder brother on a fold-up camp bed. When I started menstruating, the close proximity to my brother became awkward so he and I managed to find a mattress for me. It was discarded by the English family living in the mock Tudor houses at the top of the hill at *Atas Bukit*, which was above our kampong. In the beginning, while sleeping on the floor, I would quake with terror when the rats emerged from drains and fields to scuttle all around me in the dark, their nails scratching the crude cement floor. Even though it was hot, humid and muggy, I always had a thin blanket pulled right up to my ears in case the rats decided to keep me company in my bed! So there I was lying on this mattress, dreaming of the handsome P. Ramlee planting kisses on my cheek. I could feel the wetness of his saliva.

"Oh, Ramlee," I mouthed dreamily.

But he didn't smell as I had imagined he would smell. In fact he smelled doggy. The gamey doggy smell woke me up with a start. My parents always opened the kitchen door the moment they got up so that air could rush in to cool the house. A neighbour's dog must have inadvertently wandered through, without anyone noticing, and it was the dog who was licking my face and slobbering all over me! Yuck! My dream of P. Ramlee evaporated immediately. Alas!

I was envious that the beautiful leading ladies like Saloma and Siput Sarawak got to sing and dance with P. Ramlee. Most of the films were musicals, and P. Ramlee had a sonorous and sexy voice. Two of his most famous films were *Ibu Mertua-Ku* (*My Mother-in-Law*) and *Bujang Lapuk* (*Old Bachelor*), and he sang the eponymous songs, making everyone cry at the first and laugh at the second. Admiring fans and villagers would crowd the magnificent Alkaff Gardens whenever a film-shoot was taking place. But to my joy nobody got to kiss him either – such intimacy was not flaunted on screen in our time.

"*P. Ramlee datang! P. Ramlee datang!* P. Ramlee is here! P. Ramlee is here," the shouts would go up whenever the great actor arrived. I, like all the other young girls, would shriek and swoon at the sight of him. Many would flock to the first air-conditioned cinema, *The Alhambra* in Geylang, to see his films.

It was a treat to go to the cinema then. Mostly we watched films outdoors in a communal area when the Film-Man came with his reels of films and a portable screen. It was quite a challenge to watch films outdoors during the monsoon season! Umbrellas would go up and the screen would come down. When there was a break in the rain, the umbrellas came down and the screen went up. We learnt to keep the thread of the story in our heads whilst waiting for the rain to stop. Sometimes we would even discuss what could possibly come next. This back and forth yo-yoing would go on until the Film-Man got fed up and gave up altogether. Then we really had to make up our own endings. Probably my first training as a future writer! But when it was not rainy, it was so much fun. We sat on seats constructed out of a plank placed on top of two kerosene tins at each end. Hawkers took the opportunity to ply their wares; the *kachang putih* man sold a variety of nuts in cones made out of newspaper, the *ice-ball man* shaped the shaved ice into a ball with his naked hands, then swirled it with colourful syrup, the *mua chee* woman slicing the sesame flavoured mountain of *mua chee* with a flat aluminium slicer.

Singapore was largely rural in the 1950s. Orchard Road was still an expanse of nutmeg trees and palms. Coconut trees abounded, particularly in villages, and if they were not on a privately-owned plantation, the fruit could be plucked by anyone agile enough to climb the tall trees. Usually it was the small Malay men who could scale up the trees like monkeys, their bare hands and feet gripping the rough trunk. I have a memory of seeing one climber nearly reaching his goal. He was close to the plume of coconut leaves where all the coconuts were hanging. He reached out to pluck a coconut. Only it wasn't a coconut. It was a *tabuan,* a wasps' nest! In retaliation, the swarm of *tabuan* surrounded him and stung him. He fell from the top of the tree, falling headlong downwards, screaming as he did so.

Those were the trees where my mother got her coconuts from to make her *nasi lemak.* But usually it was coconuts she had *found*, brought down by the wind. It was amazing what one could find when one was poor and hungry – a chicken's egg from a hen that had strayed from its coop: an eel, *belot,* from the monsoon drains; *ubi kayu,* or tapioca, from the undergrowth of forests; fallen fruits from over-hanging branches from people's gardens; half-eaten cakes and boiled sweets from the dustbins of the rich English.

It was a laborious task to separate the coconut husk from its shell; then to scrape the moist white flesh out; then manually grating the kernel on a metal grater, and finally adding water to squeeze out the milk. But the result was worth all that effort. I can still taste Mak's special coconut rice in my memory as if time has not passed.

The Kallang River cut a broad swathe across Kampong Potong Pasir. This river was both the boon and bane of the village. It caused major floods in 1954 and 1967. In the days when there was no piped water supply to the kampong, its water and surrounding springs and wells provided drinking water. Vegetable farms grew up on the banks of the river, farmed by Chinese farmers, supplying fresh *chyesim, kailan,* water cress, *ubi kayu* to markets around the island. I can still remember fooling around with the neighbourhood kids in our bare feet on the mud bunds that surrounded the *padi* fields. It was simply a delightful experience to squelch our toes into cool, wet clay and mud.

Before I was ten, I was like a boy, bare-chested and flat-chested, dressed only in homemade drawstring shorts. My mother was an expert on the *Singer*-sewing machine. During Chinese New Year, she would peddle it furiously. Like all Peranakans, she was *pantang,* superstitious, and insisted on new curtains for the house and new clothes for us, to bring in good luck and prosperity. Unable to afford fabric from the major department stores, *Robinson's* or *Metro* or stores on the High Street, she would buy them from peddlers at *Robinson Petang* (Thieves Market) at Sungei Road. Because most of the goods sold were either stolen or damaged property, it was pure luck whether we got fabric that would be the same shade the whole way through! When times were really bad and she could not afford to buy any new clothes for us, she would recycle the previous year's curtains, to sew them into shirts and dresses. At least the clothes were regarded as new!

"So clever your mother!" Neighbours would say when they saw all of us eight brothers and sisters wearing clothes in the same patterned material. But my brothers were not amused; floral patterns were not masculine enough for shirts!

I was born in 1951 and spent all of my childhood and teenage years in Kampong Potong Pasir. Lighting was provided by carbide and hurricane lamps and later, a generator supplied intermittent electricity. It was pot-luck when the generator worked, making for some exciting times.

My mother's *nasi lemak* and her skill in making *nonya kueh* rescued me from a life of ignorance. Without them and her tremendous effort to defy my father and, against all odds, to enrol me in school, I might have been someone's maid, or running a foodstall selling *nasi lemak* all my life instead of writing these English words. My moment of epiphany came when I saw a Milo tin when I was around seven or eight. It suddenly hit me that I could not understand the squiggles that were inscribed on the tin.

"Mak, I want to go to school," I said.

"You know that your father won't allow it or pay for it."

"But I want to study, learn English."

"How badly do you want to go to school?"

"I really, really want to."

"How really is really? Are you prepared to work for it?"

I noticed that her eyes lit up. I was her first surviving daughter. There were others before me who had not lived due to the lack of food and health-care. She had so many children, she lost count.

"It would be good if you don't have to depend on a man for your living all your life. I have to put up with a lot. You need not go through what I have to. I will take in the neighbours' washing and you can help me wash the clothes, bringing the water up from the well. I will make more *nonya kueh* and *nasi lemak* and you can go round the village selling them."

"Yes, yes!" I said with enthusiasm. "I will do anything to go to school!"

And so I followed in my brother's footsteps and hawked the *nasi lemak* around the kampong. "*Nasi Lemak! Nasi Lemak! Sepuloh Sen!* Coconut Rice! Coconut Rice!" But by this time, the price had gone up to ten cents per packet.

Growing up in the kampong, we were deprived of many comforts. Our family was extremely poor. There were days when we did not have any food to eat. Some days it was just soya sauce on boiled broken rice, the lowest quality rice which was used as feed for chickens. But the greatest thing we had was our mother's love. She was a special lady, beautiful, devoted, compassionate and inspirational, not just to our family but to all the other villagers. She motivated each one of us to work hard and to succeed. My brothers and sisters all became successful in their chosen careers and businesses, buying themselves landed properties. I was the least business-minded, starting off as an Assistant Dental Nurse for seven years, then I attended *Lembaga*, adult education classes, to sit for my A-Levels. Eventually I managed to get into Singapore University; the first in my family to do so. I read literature, for I had dreamt (considered silly at that time) of becoming a writer. Having a family and a career postponed my dream for sometime, but eventually I decided that it was what I really wanted to spend my life doing. I managed to do an MA in a Creative Writing programme at a university in England.

In 1992, I became the first Singaporean to be short-listed for one of the UK's top literary awards for short stories, the Ian St. James Award. I wish my mother had been present at the award ceremony at the London Hilton. One of my sisters did attend to share my joy. Subsequently, I was invited to appear as a local author at literary events in the south-east of England. It was a great accolade. I could not have achieved my dream if Mak had not sacrificed so much. Thus, I am eternally indebted to her.

Kampong Potong Pasir was razed to the ground in the early 1970s. The village metamorphosed into a concrete Housing Development Board (HDB) estate. The broad Kallang River was narrowed, some of its water channelled elsewhere. All the vegetable farms were dug up and the fish ponds filled. And we lost some magnificent trees like the *angsana* and *banyan*, with their splendid canopy of leaves. A foundation of drainage and water systems was necessary for the creation of the blocks of flats, so the land was raised to its present level. So what used to be a hill at *Atas Bukit* now looks like a small bump. In fact there may have been more hills in this area in the old days because the words *potong pasir* mean to *cut sand* – *potong* means *cut* and *pasir* is *sand*. In Hokkien it is called *Suah Ti*. *Suah* means *sand*. *Ti* refers to the *fish ponds.* Some of these ponds were created when sand was excavated for land reclamation.

Like many kampongs in Singapore, our village too was destroyed in the 1970s. Bull dozers stampeded in like a herd of mechanical beasts flattening the attap houses, consigning our way of life into history books. So I cannot *balik kampong. Balik kampong* in Malay literally means *going back (to the) village* but it is also a metaphor that suggests a kind of emotional going home. I can no longer *balik kampong*, at least not in a physical sense. But I can always return to it in my memory and would like to share these memories with you.

Alkaff Gardens, 1930s.
Although this photo was actually taken in the 1930s,
it was still quite similar in the 1950s. (Courtesy of Lim Kheng Chye)

View of a vegetable farm at Potong Pasir, 1950s.
(From the National Archives)

First younger sister posing in front of a
colonial black and white Tudor house at *Atas Bukit*, 1968.

Days Of Darkness
(1955)

NEARLY EVERY MEMORY I have of my childhood is connected with my mother. She was such a philosophical lady. One does not need a university degree to be philosophical. The ancient Greeks tell us that the word philosophy can be broken up into *philo*, which means *love of* and *Sophia*, which means *wisdom*. So someone who spouts wise sayings can be philosophical, but wisdom need not always be intellectual and acquired. It can be intuitive. Mak was a wise woman indeed. She was uneducated like most women of her time in that she was not literate. But she was certainly educated by the University of Life. My strongest memory of her is her genteel manner and the amazing wisdom that spouted from her lips. I may not recall all her sayings in the exact way she said them but I certainly believe I have captured the essence of what she said.

"It's not where you live that counts but *how* you live," she used to say.

This would be great if you were living in comfort and luxury but when you were like me, a child in *Kampong Potong Pasir*, where you had to live among rats scuttling along the cement floor or centipedes falling off the attap roof, you would have wondered if my mother's philosophy was for real. But she *was* for real. I can say with my hand on my heart that she was the most influential person in my life. It was her positive philosophy and attitude that nurtured me and set me up for as long as I may live.

I was born in March 1951. The year of my birth was auspicious for the island of Singapore and its people. In September that year, it was proclaimed a City by the British. In later years, I heard stories of how the *Padang* had so many people celebrating the momentous occasion that the field of grass which gave it its name was blocked from view. Laughter and cries of joy burst out when the fireworks erupted in a myriad of colours above the Esplanade, which was then a tree-lined walkway by the sea. To crown the event, an illuminated dragon-float glided across the seafront to the delight of everyone present. So my birth was also the birth of a hope for independence for our nation.

By the time I was three, people were crying out, "We want Self-rule! We want Self-rule!"

Just as I was about to turn four, the country was caught in election fever.

"We want our own local leader!" People cried out to the British rulers.

Our village was a hive of excitement. Our *kampong* road had never seen such a parade of vehicles, vans and open-topped lorries, trundling down its pot-holed lanes, their wheels raising clouds of dust. The party leaders shouted political slogans and promises from hand-held megaphones. There was David Marshall, from the Labour Front Party, Lee Kuan Yew from the newly formed People's Action Party, and even an independent candidate, Ahmad Ibrahim. Great crowds of people rallied around them, inspiring everyone with their messages.

"We want to improve your lives," they said. "We will provide you with running water and electricity, and food to quiet your rumbling stomachs."

Villages like ours were served by wells, and we had no running water in the houses. Usually the stand-pipe, which provided drinking water, was some distance away. The electricity in the city did not reach our homes. Our homes were lit by hurricane lamps, kerosene or carbide lamps and candles. And the majority of villagers were poor and uneducated. The political candidates played on our lack of education, obliquely persuading us that the colonial government did not have our interests at heart but that local government would. We were motivated to act from hunger and to be free from the squalor of our everyday living. So villagers turned out *en masse* on polling day, April 2, to vote. David Marshall won a narrow victory and became our country's first chief minister. Sadly his Labour Front Government was jinxed; a strike took place soon after he took office, and there were many more after that.

That particular strike was by the Hock Lee Amalgamated Bus Company. Two anti-colonists, Fong Swee Suan and Lim Chin Siong, who were the leaders of The Singapore Bus Workers Union, were reported to incite their members, saying "You are deluded if you think that the Labour Party is not being controlled by the Colonial Government. Don't be deceived. This government is only a pawn for the British! What have they done for you, eh? What? You work day and night and you still get so little pay and have not enough to eat. You live in villages that have no running water or electricity, where sanitation is appalling and disease rampant. We want better terms and conditions!"

Indeed, bus drivers and conductors, Ah Chye, Peng An, Salleh and Gurjit were from rural villages like ours. They had experienced the devastating flood that had hit Potong Pasir the previous year, in 1954. Houses in the kampong were made with wooden walls and palm-thatched attap roofs. So they were flimsy and could not withstand the heavy monsoon and surging flood waters. Many people became homeless or lost possessions. Therefore in villages like ours, people were looking for a saviour to remove our deprivations and give us a better life. Lowly paid folks like Ah Chye, Peng An, Salleh and Gurjit decided to join the strikers in the hope that they could provide more for their families.

"Our pay is too low!" The strikers shouted, together with all the others, raising a thicket of fists into the air. "We can't feed our wives and children or buy shoes for them. We work very long hours in terrible conditions yet our stomachs still rumble!"

On May 12, an event which came to be known as *Black Thursday* devastated the country. Nearly 2,000 students from Chinese Middle Schools joined the strikers of the Hock Lee Bus Company. Students from Chinese schools were disgruntled with the colonial government because their education was not recognised. Also they were not permitted to get into the University of Malaya even when they had the right qualifications.

The strikers caused a major riot in Alexandra Road and Tiong Bahru. They barricaded the depots and stopped the buses from leaving the depots. Wives and mothers like Ah Sum, Ah Moey, Khatija and Gita from our village took out their *tingkat* or tiffin carriers. These were two- or three-tiered food containers, the enamel ones painted with brightly coloured flowers and birds. The steel ones were plain or carved. Mothers and wives filled these with delicious food to take to their husbands and sons behind the picket line. They had to walk miles, as the city's transport system had ground to a halt. Only those with private cars or who could afford taxis and *pawang chiar* could still travel comfortably.

"*Aiiyah!* Eat something-*lah!*" Ah Sum persuaded her husband.

Students from the Chinese schools brought food and even entertained the workers by singing and dancing. Had it remained a peaceful strike, no one would have been hurt. The police tried to break them up with water cannons and tear gas, so both strikers and students retaliated, with devastating results. Ah Moey came back to the village distraught and in tears.

"What happened? What happened?" Neighbours asked her.

"*Sway, sway-lah!* Misfortune, misfortune-*lah*. My husband, Peng An. His head was smashed by a police truncheon. He's in hospital now."

It was indeed a day of darkness.

Across the Kallang River from our village was an English Missionary School, Saint Andrew's School, which was run by a man called Canon Reginald Keith Sorby Adams. He had been nicknamed *The Fighting Padre* as it was he who introduced boxing as a sport to the school. He was one of the few Europeans or white men seen around our village, handing out alms or just being friendly. Besides this English missionary school was a Chinese school in Kampong Potong Pasir. Unlike St. Andrew's, which was built of concrete, the Chinese school was an open wooden hut with wooden flooring, its roof thatched with attap. The pupils sat on long wooden benches facing an old-fashioned blackboard which the teacher would scratch with his white chalk. The colonial government did not fund Chinese education, so that opened the sluice gates of opportunity for the communists to spread their influence. China sent teachers, school-books and funds, purportedly to educate their Chinese nationals abroad. Most of the pupils in our village school were from *Lai Par*, the inner sanctum of Kampong Potong Pasir where their parents tilled the earth and grew vegetables.

"*Yi, Er, San, Si* ... One, Two, Three, Four..."

Mandarin was not spoken in our part of the village except at that school. Chinese people in our village mostly spoke Teochew or Hokkien and some Cantonese. The other village children, including myself, would crowd round the school listening to this foreign language. Apparently it was this language that linked the local Chinese to their Motherland and it was this sentiment that the communist insurgents played upon. People liked to belong somewhere and at this point in time, Singapore still felt like a staging post, not yet its own nation. The different immigrant races still thought of their former countries as their Motherlands. However, Peranakans, because of their mixed heritage, have an affiliation to China but consider Malaya as their home. At this point in history, the word, *Malaya* was used interchangeably to include Singapore, and did not merely refer to the Federated States of Malaya. That was why the first university in our country was called the University of Malaya.

It was through schools like those in our village that the communists spelled out their mission to overthrow the Colonial government. In our innocence, the village children and I spied on the school. The lessons were carried out in a sing-song manner with lots of rote learning, where the pupils repeated again and again what the teacher taught. If the teacher was male, he'd wear a short-sleeved white shirt with navy-blue trousers. If the teacher was female, she'd wear a cheongsam, and her face was severely framed with a straight page-boy haircut.

"Why fight for them?" the communists had mooted to impressionable teenagers who were on the cusp of being drafted into National Service the previous year. "Where were they in our country's time of need? They deserted us and let the Japanese walk in. Isn't it time that we threw the British out?"

But of course, I was too little to know anything of the social unrest or political stirrings. All I knew was, I was not comfortable with the strange-sounding Mandarin language. I was comfortable with Malay and our Baba patois, which was Malay mixed or *champur* with Hokkien and Teochew. Like all children, my only concern was for my own welfare in my own little world.

Despite the fact that my family had difficulty getting our quota of food and vitamins for each day, I had a luxuriant head of hair like my mother. But unlike my mother's, mine was so straight it sprung out from my head like a stiff broomstick, the kind of broomstick which we used to make from the spine of coconut leaves, called *sapu lidi*. We collected bunches of coconut leaves, then shaved the green parts of the leaf until only the spine remained. The spines were dried in the sun until they browned, when we tied them together with jute strings to make a broom. It was perfect for sweeping up sandy yards, like those at the back of our attap house where banana, papaya and angsana trees grew. But when my hair grew long, it softened and when plaited, it was manageable. There was so much of it, hanging like a black curtain down my back and I became so proud of it. But *Pride goeth before a fall*. I am sure you have heard the saying. It was my first big lesson in life.

One of my most pleasurable memories is of my mother combing my long hair. When the sun beat down mercilessly, our zinc roofed kitchen became a sweltering oven, so we would cool ourselves by sitting on the threshold of our house trying to catch the breeze that passed. I usually sat in the cradle of her knees and she would run a multi-toothed comb again and again through my hair till it shone. The *lorongs* or passages between the rows of houses were so narrow that if you stretched your legs out, you could touch the legs of the neighbours sitting opposite on their threshold.

"Ei Nonya," Mak Ahyee, our neighbour asked. She like everyone in the village, addressed my mother with the Peranakan term for a lady, *nonya*. "What oil do you use for her hair?"

"Coconut milk. Freshly squeezed from grated coconut," Mak said. "I put it on her head and allow it to soak through into the hair for an hour to condition it."

"So beautiful. So beautiful!"

Mak deftly plaited my hair into two thick plaits. And then I went off to play with the rest of the kampong children. We were an assortment of Malay, Indian, Punjabi, Eurasian and Chinese young people of various ages. Many of the children were not educated, so our common language was Malay.

"*Hari ini kita main chapteh.* Today we'll play *chapteh,*" Abu said. He was the elder bother of my friend, Fatima. He was only twelve but always styled himself the leader. If my big brothers were at home, they took the part. But Abu had a certain *je ne sais quoi* that made him a natural leader.

Some people could afford store-bought *chaptehs* with a thick rubber base and plumes of colourful feathers. But we hardly ever bought toys from stores. If we were lucky, the English families living at the top of the hill at *Atas Bukit* (literally meaning *on-top-of-hill*) would throw out their children's unwanted toys. Sometimes they were broken, other times, just a little bit damaged and if we were extremely lucky, only because they were old. Their rubbish bins became our treasure troves. Sometimes we even salvaged uneaten food from them: a half-eaten banana or apple, left-over cake, boiled sweets which had melted into their wrappers. But English children did not play *chapteh.* So we had to learn to make our own. With a flourish, Abu produced one that he had made.

"*Wah!!!*" All the children exclaimed at its magnificence.

He had cut rubber circles from disused car-tyres and nailed them together. On the spikes of the nails, he had impaled several feathers. The feathers looked fresh, as if they had just been plucked recently from a chicken or duck, and perhaps one from a *mynah* bird. Abu was not opposed to pursuing a chicken to pluck its feathers. I could imagine him chasing the distraught chicken as it clucked and raced around in mindless circles out of sheer panic. Round the base of the quills, he had strapped jute string to hold everything together.

"The rule is," he pronounced authoritatively. "You can only kick it with the sole of your foot. Otherwise you are out! The person who keeps it in the air longest with the most number of kicks wins."

"Can I use my left foot?" One of the other boys asked.

Village children hardly ever wore any footwear. If we had to visit the filthy outhouses, we would put on our wooden clogs, called *char kiak* in Hokkien, *terompah* in Malay. They were the must-have items in kampongs. The stocky *char kiaks* were usually made with an inch or more thickness, so you felt taller when you were wearing them. It was the platform footwear of the fifties. They were very functional, as they served the purpose of keeping feet dry and clean when traversing puddles and fly-riddled cow-pats, which were numerous in the villages. There was a *char kiak* shop in our village where the craftsmen shaved wooden blocks by hand to fashion them into clogs. If you passed the shop, you could smell the aromatic smell of fresh wood and see wood shavings on the dirt floor, plus stacks of unvarnished clogs waiting to be painted. *Char kiaks* came in bright colours like red and yellow, with matching coloured plastic straps. When you walked in them on a cement or concrete street or floor, the clogs made a characteristic sound, *clok, clok clok*; hence its English onomatopoeic name. You could never creep up on someone undetected! When rubber flip-flops came into fashion, people opted for them because they were less cumbersome and less noisy.

"Left foot. Right foot. I don't care. As long as it's your *tapak kaki*. The *sole* of your foot." Abu emphasised.

I was one of the few girls who joined in games with the boys. I was a boy at heart, even at that young age, wanting to do adventurous things, wanting *not* to be restricted to activities merely of my gender. Because I was so little, they humoured me and allowed me to play. But I kicked up sand and dust and even more dust while they laughed at my futile attempts.

But I enjoyed playing with the girls too. Although Fatima and I got on well, my best friend was really Parvathi, an Indian girl three years older than myself. We loved *masak-masak* – the word literally meant *cooking* but it was a game of make-believe, pretending that we were grown-up women making a home, cooking, having babies. But sadly, Parvathi never made it to womanhood, nor had a real baby. I have told her story, which contains a vital lesson, in the chapter *"Dying to be Free."*

Our *pretend-babies* were fashioned out of old rags or straw. Some of our *babies* were handicapped, lacking an eye or a limb; they were the dolls we rescued from the bins at *Atas Bukit*. But we took care of them; we bathed, dressed and fed them. We were training to be real mothers, never rejecting our children no matter what condition they were in. Engrossed in making cakes from mud and drinks from drain-water, our clothes became dirty, our hair and faces matted with dirt. Sometimes in digging around in the sand, we encountered squiggly earth-worms and we squealed in fright. The boys were amused but usually took these from us to use them as bait to catch fish or *belot*, eels, in the river or mud-banks. The main river that ran through Kampong Potong Pasir – the Kallang River. – used to be much broader than it is today, with water swelling during the monsoon periods, flooding its banks. Eels made their homes in its moist banks. Since many kampong folk could not afford to buy food, they had to find it in the countryside: eels, fish from the river, birds' eggs, *ubi kayu* or tapioca and coconut that grew in the wilderness.

A good Peranakan cook like my mother could make delicious meals out of most things. Peranakan girls were taught to cook at an early age. Mak's best eel dish was cooked in *rempah*, a rich but dry curry paste. She would cut the eel into slices, marinate them with turmeric and chilli powder, then fry each piece. This took away the sliminess that was often associated with fresh eels. Then she pounded fresh chillies, onions, garlic, ginger, coriander and cumin seeds in her *batu lesong* or rolled them on her granite *batu gilling* to make them into a thick paste. She would sauté the curry paste in the *kwali* over the coal fire till the fragrance filled the air and made our mouths water. She'd squeeze milk out of a coconut but used only the first press called *pati-santan* and added this to the thick curry. Then she'd slip the cooked eels into this sauce and allow the sauce to thicken and coat the eel slices. Eaten with boiled rice, this was absolutely delicious and was a feast for us!

Of course, playing in the sand, we picked up germs. And other things too. But we were never very concerned about things like that. Well, I was not concerned. Not until my scalp started to itch. I scratched and scratched and scratched.

"Stop scratching your head. All your hair will fall out!" Mak admonished.

But I did not stop. The itching became so intense, I started to cry.

"Come here!" She said. "Let me look."

She let out a yelp.

"*Kutu! Kutu!* " She shouted in horror. "Lice! Lice! My God, you're infested!"

So she waged war on them. She parted each section of my hair, ferreted out the little mites and squeezed them between her thumb and finger. Each louse departed its mortal life with an explosion of pungent odour. The smell made me want to throw up so I howled some more. Serve me right for being so proud of my beautiful hair!

We could not afford posh things like *Palmolive soap* and shampoos then, though we dreamed of their creamy softness when we looked at advertisements in posters and women's magazines like *Her World*. But they were beyond our reach. We had to wash our hair and our body with the same *Sunlight* cake soap that Mak used for washing the clothes. For more stubborn stains, she used a black cake of carbolic soap that smelled foul. She dragged me to our communal bathroom, a rectangular wooden wall with a concrete floor that surrounded a well, the top open to the sky. It never made sense to me to bathe on rainy days when it would do just as well to stand in the rain outside.

"Sit!" She ordered.

Mak drew up several buckets of water, careful not to draw up the two catfish that were put down the well to eat up mosquitoes. Fortunately, due to the recent rain, the water was clear. During the dry months, one would draw up thick muddy water. It was not a joy to bathe during that period. Then we would make the trek to a local spring the kampong folks called *Pipe Besar*. Mak tipped the water into a *baldi*, a steel oval-shaped bucket with a ridge underfoot. After wetting my hair, she scrubbed and scrubbed my head with the carbolic soap. It hurt.

"Ow! Ow! Ow!" I went.

"Keep still! Would you rather keep all these lice in your hair?"

But even after all her strenuous efforts, the lice still proliferated.

"Okay no choice now," Mak said. "It's the kerosene treatment for you."

"Oh, no Mak, please, no!"

I had seen Mak Ah Yee treat her daughter Ah Yee with the kerosene treatment, and it was awful. The whole scalp was doused with kerosene. It was obviously a folk remedy that must have produced the desired results.

My mother was a determined lady.

Kerosene came in a rectangular metal container and it was used to fuel kerosene stoves, although Mak still preferred to cook on her clay stove with coals. When Mak poured some into an enamel mug, its fumes rose to my nostrils. I nearly retched. My mother forced me to sit still and placed a towel around my shoulders. You know what it is like when someone forces something on you, telling you that it is for your own good though you hate every minute of it. That was what it was like, me sitting with my head bowed as she rinsed my whole head of hair with the stuff. It felt yucky and it stank. Where I had scratched my scalp previously, the kerosene made the scalp sting.

"Sit there for an hour or so," she said. "The kerosene should murder the lice!"

I was utterly miserable.

Even at that tender age, I had a wild imagination. What if someone threw a lighted match in my direction? My head could be set alight like Moses' burning bush! No divine revelation there, or the voice of God, just me screaming in sheer agony. That would make my mother feel sorry for me. It would certainly roast the little buggers in my hair!

But my misery was nothing compared to that of families caught in the strikes and riots. Altogether there were 275 strikes in 1955. Every now and again, adults would shout out warnings and the children were ushered indoors in haste. Our wooden windows would be shuttered and doors urgently bolted. We cowered behind our wooden walls and listened to the stampede of rushing feet running past our doors. Trouble-makers and rioters often sought refuge in kampongs because of the maze of *lorongs* that tended to confuse the uninitiated, like the English policemen. In 1950, when the Maria Hertogh affair caused the Muslims to retaliate against the colonial government, many of the rioters sought refuge in the kampongs. More often than not, the colonial police were reluctant to enter local villages because the rioters or trouble-makers often had their supporters lying in wait in the kampongs. The sympathisers would stand in menacing groups, wielding agrarian weapons of destruction like *parangs* (machete-looking knives) and *cangkuls* (hoes). Kampong Tai Seng, near Paya Lebar, was notorious for harbouring rioters, hardened criminals and gangsters.

My own black day came when my mother decided to cut off my long hair. I was too young to appreciate the blackness of what had just taken place in the country, though I was not too young to imbibe the sense of tension that arose from it. *The Straits Times* reported it for weeks. Adults in our village talked about it for days on end, clustering in the narrow *lorongs* or under the spread of angsana trees. We followed bus-driver Peng An's progress in hospital and rejoiced with Ah Moey when her husband finally came home, even though on crutches, his head bandaged. Ah Moey had thought he would not live. But my childish focus did not extend further than myself.

Mak came toward me like a malevolent creature with her scissors.

"It's for your own good," she said, as I tried to escape her. "Less hair means less *kutu!*"

As she snipped, my long hair spiralled downwards to our cement floor. I wept. When I looked in the mirror afterwards and saw my mutilated hair, I howled.

"You're so wicked! Wicked! Wicked! Wicked!"

It is the only recollection I have of saying something nasty to my mother.

Normally if we said anything rude or nasty, we would get the *sumbat sambal belachan* treatment. It was a torture worse than hell for us kids. The intense heat and sting of the *chilli-padi*, the hottest chilli in South East Asia, would make you leap up and down like a crazed monkey. That's why Peranakans have a saying, *macham monyet kena sambal belachan, like a monkey who had eaten prawn-chilli paste.* The trouble was that drinking gallons of cold water only made the agony worse! Mak would pound her *sambal belachan*, or shrimp paste, with hot *chilli-padi*, and *sumbat* or stuff it into our mouths so we would never utter any bad words again. The *rotan*, the cane, was not the only way our parents disciplined us! But this time, she was kinder. She must have felt sorry for my loss as well, because she tried to appease me. She cooked her best *bubor kachang*, mung beans in coconut milk with pandan leaves. Its fragrant wafting aroma made me forget my distress. It was easy to tempt me.

On August 20, excitement was in the air.

"*Chepat! Chepat!* Come quick!" Abu called out. "*Kapal Terbang*! Aeroplane!"

We heard it too, the throbbing engine of the aeroplane flying overhead – as rare a sound and sight as a motor-car coming into our village. Children and adults raced out into the open yard to look overhead.

"It's going to the new airport at Paya Lebar," my father, Ah Tetia, said with authority. "The Secretary of State for Colonies, Mr Alan Lennox-Boyd, is officiating at the opening."

My father was a bill-collector with a British firm, thus he spoke some English and he pronounced the English name with aplomb. The other villagers looked up at him in awe.

The Malay word *paya* meant *swamp*, and *lebar* meant *wide*. Paya Lebar was on the Eastern side of the island and was connected to our village by the Kallang River. My father had taken me past a swamp at *Toa Payoh*, the Hokkien name meaning the same as *Paya Lebar* in Malay. I recall the swamp's sinister look, acres of thick, dark mud, surrounded by mangrove trees with their aerial roots, which in the half-light looked like monsters stretching out arms and long fingers. Deep-throated frogs burped sonorously across the eerie landscape. To build the new airport to replace Kallang Airport, the villages surrounding the swamp were relocated to the North of the island. As the villagers were mostly Chinese who raised pigs that were taboo to Malays, those villages were called Chinese Kampongs.

"If you are good," Ah Tetia said to me. "I will take you to the airport to see the new passenger terminal."

Indeed, he did fulfil his promise. I had such complex and mixed feelings about my father. He could be so volatile and bad-tempered. Yet I have stored wonderful memories of his tenderness.

That same year, my father's fourth younger brother and his wife, who lived in Petain Road near the city, invited us to their home for Christmas. Fourth Uncle had to be addressed as *Si Chik*, and Fourth Aunty had to be called *Si Sim*. This manner of calling was very precise, so even a stranger could decipher the exact relationship of the person being addressed to the person making the address, which side of the family the uncle and aunt were from and which rung they occupied in the family; not like the modern *Uncle* and *Aunty* people use these days. In my perception, Si Chik and Si Sim were rich, as they lived in the city in an apartment block, which had running water and electricity. It was a treat to visit them as we could use their toilet, which was clean and not smelly, unlike our *jambans* or outhouses. Plus it had a flush system. It seemed like magic to me that when you pulled a chain, water sluiced out to wash your mess away. To wipe their bottoms, they had a roll of loo-paper, white, soft and clean, compared to the squares of newspaper we had to use. When caught in the rain whilst queuing to use our outhouses, our newspaper squares would get soggy and when we wiped our bottoms, the newsprint would come off and smear our bottoms with black ink!

My aunt and uncle had two daughters, Mary, who was the same age as me, and her sister, Janet, who was three years younger; and the youngest was a boy. As Mary and I were only months apart, I was constantly compared to her.

"Look at Mary, she's so white and pretty. How come you're so black? So ugly! No one will marry you!" My father said.

I can recall the young Mary clearly, with her fair skin and up-turned nose, which sniffed at conditions in our kampong when she was forced to visit at Chinese New Year. She and Janet would be in beautiful Metro-bought dresses. Metro was our local department store in the High Street, but my family could not afford any items from there. My cousins wore shiny black patent shoes and lacy socks. They were so conscious of catching something that they refused to take their shoes off. Instead they walked into our attap-hut with their shoes on. It was taboo on normal days to wear shoes in the house, and it was worse on Chinese New Year Day. But despite their father's cajoling, they refused to take their shoes off. My aunt never visited us as she too could not bear to visit our village. I knew that my mother was pained by her attitude.

"I've got some money from *chap ji ki*," Mak said. Like most women in the village, she indulged in a bit of gambling with the prospect of winning a windfall. The harmless gambling gave hope when circumstances were dire. The other money-accruing device that villagers indulged in was their contribution to tontine, or *senoman* in Malay. The latter was a kind of communal saving scheme, each person in the scheme taking turns to collect the entire pool of money when their need was paramount.

"We'll do something nice to your hair, shall we? Wouldn't it be good for your cousins to see we can afford to have your hair permed?"

Maybe she was also trying to make amends for cutting off my long, beautiful hair. Though this was a new technology, permanent waves were becoming fashionable. European women magazines featured beautiful ladies with curly hair, some even blonde or brunette. Black and white films, with a cute little American called Shirley Temple who had dimples and gorgeous ringlets, were popular. All the village kids, myself included, could not wait for the Film-Man to bring us a Shirley Temple film. He would screen it outdoors whilst we sat on make-shift wooden benches. Every little girl wanted to have Shirley Temple's dimples and soft curls. Little girls believed that they could get dimples if they stuck their finger into their cheeks. So you could spy children in the village spending hours poking their fingers into their cheeks! I was lucky to be born with dimples in both cheeks, but my hair was straight and rigid. As it happened, a salon had opened just on the outskirts of Kampong Potong Pasir. Mak herself always had her hair long and straight, tied up in a bun like most Peranakan and Malay women. But she wanted me to be modern. Like many mothers, she liked to treat me like her doll. I was her eldest living daughter, her other daughters had died before I was born. My sister, who was two years younger than me could not have her hair waved yet. I thought of myself looking pretty like Shirley Temple and I was excited by Mak's suggestion.

The acrid smell of ammonia hit me as we entered the small salon. There were tall mirrors on one side of the room and women sitting in chairs, wrapped in black capes. There were posters of the beautiful Chinese actresses Lin Dai and Huang Li Li, their complexions as white as porcelain, considered by the Chinese to be the epitome of beauty. That was why I was always considered ugly as I was too black. Mak spoke to the hairdresser, her voice low and sweet as it always was.

"I'll be back later to pick you up," she said to me reassuringly.

I was made to sit on a high stool, my legs dangling off the floor.

The hairdresser talked above my head to the other ladies as she worked with my short hair, soaking it with the permanent wave lotion. It smelled foul and I nearly retched. It was worse than the kerosene Mak had used. I was beginning to regret having my hair permed. To console myself, I made myself think of sweet Shirley Temple and how I was going to look like her. The hairdresser took each section of my hair and curled it round a metal rod which was attached to a wire. By the time she was finished, I was like Medusa, snakes of electrical cable emerging from my head. The weight of it was immeasurable. It made my neck ache and gave me a severe headache. To my horror, the hairdresser switched on the power and the rods grew hotter and hotter – my face felt like it was slowly being cooked. The heat burned through my scalp. This was what it would have felt like if someone had indeed thrown a lighted match my way when my head was doused with kerosene! But it was not the lice which were roasting, it was me! I hugged myself so as not to cry.

It was a relief when the power was finally turned off and the heavy load was taken off my head. When my hair was released from the rods, it sprang up in all directions as if I had been electrified. The hairdresser was definitely a novice at perming hair! My new hairdo was horrible and I hated it. When my mother came back and saw me, all she said was, "*Alamak!*"

The hairdresser looked embarrassed. She whispered something to my mother. But she could not offer any remedies. My hair was so strong that the botched perm stayed petrified till Christmas.

I sulked as my parents took my sister and me to town to visit my aunt and uncle who lived with *Lao Ee*, my paternal grandmother. I couldn't understand why she was addressed in the Teochew term of *Old Aunt* from the maternal side of the family, but she was worth visiting. Plus the other pleasure I got from visiting them was that I could use their toilet. Even at that age, I had the sheer tenacity and capacity of saving my bowel movement till I got to their flat – which was quite a feat! But I already suffered a severe identity crisis whenever we met my cousins because everyone said how pretty cousin Mary was because she was so white, and I was so ugly because I was so black. Apparently the Chinese have no word for brown or tanned! Now I had to meet them with my hair looking like I had stuck my head in an oven!

"Oh *rambut pendek*! Oh short hair. New hairdo, huh?" Lao Ee said kindly.

Grandmother was always sweet and gentle. She often sneaked a few cents to me when no one was looking. She kept her clothes in moth-balls to protect them, so when Lao Ee hugged me, she always smelled of moth-balls or of the Tiger Balm she used. I was always curious about the hard wooden pillow which she used to rest her head on. Grandmother wore the *kebaya panjang* like most Peranakan women her age. The kebaya was longer, hence its name, *panjang*, and was much looser and more comfortable than the short kebaya, so that a less-than-perfect figure could be tastefully disguised. Once her *sanggul* or chignon was thick and black; and on festive occasions, she would decorate it with ornate hairpins, or *chochok sanggul* in our language. But these days her small and thin *sanggul* was a sad reminder of her advanced years. Lao Ee did not make any negative comment about my hair.

But I was so conscious of my botched perm. I did not want to be seen, so I hid behind my mother's sarong. I wanted the floor to open and swallow me whole. I'd rather be anywhere than at my cousins' home. I hung my head in sheer despair, biting my lower lip so that I would not cry. I had to meet my fate.

When my young cousins saw me, they laughed hysterically.

Poultry Farmer (1960).
This is similar to the type of poultry farms in Kampong Potong Pasir.
(From the National Archives)

The author, Phine, as child *before* her hair was permed.

A miserable a four-year-old Phine *after* her hair was permed – on Boxing Day (1955).

Clarion Call Of Hope
(1956)

Tɪᴋ-Tᴏᴋ, Tɪᴋ-Tᴏᴋ. The *Mee Man* clacked his bamboo clappers together loudly. The sound carried in the rural quietness of our village and roused us from our midday stupor. When the sun poured down its heat from directly overhead, it produced a somnambulistic effect on all of us. Even the chickens stopped their relentless scratching of the sand to dig up earthworms. But at the sound of the wooden clackers, people and domestic animals became alert, heads turned towards the sound, and the dogs' ears went up like periscopes.

Generally we hardly heard any mechanical noise, as there was no electricity in Kampong Potong Pasir that would bring in the sound of lawnmowers or refrigerators. Even the drone of motorcars was a rarity, since transport was provided by bicycles, trishaws or bullock carts. But we would get an occasional burst of music from battery radios and the *Rediffusion*, a cable network that was transmitted via batteries and wires. In the mornings, we awakened to birds singing, cocks crowing, dogs barking, whilst men coughed and spat to clear their throats. The sound we heard in the village just as the sun was setting was the sound of the chattering starlings as they flew back to the trees to roost. Hens and ducks would cluck and quack as they settled into the beds of straw in their wooden coops. As darkness fell, there would be sounds of villagers pumping up their hurricane lamps, or the hissing sound of carbide lamps. There was also the clatter of enamel dishes as dinner was served on concrete floors as few villagers owned dining tables. These sounds stay etched in the folds of my memory. But the one sound that remains uppermost in my memory is the sound of the clacking of the noodle-man's bamboo clackers.

Tik-Tok, Tik-Tok. The sound was a clarion call of hope for the hungry, for we knew that Ah Seng's noodles were the best. Ah Seng, dressed in his singlet and shorts, peddled his noodles in a tricycle cart, which was loaded with a boiling cauldron of soup. In the cart were Chinese white bowls with their dark blue design, chopsticks and a variety of noodles with ingredients like pork slices and fish cakes. He even carried several low wooden stools so that his customers could sit by his travelling stall. When business was good, he might give a young child the job of clapping the bamboo clappers to herald his coming. Its clapping was associated with delicious food and roused people from inertia and whetted their appetites. The child also helped him retrieve his noodle-bowls after customers had finished their meal. There was no talk of child labour or exploitation during those years; if parents could not afford to send their child to school, it meant the child had to work for a living.

"*Mee Tng*, ten cents! *Tah Mee*, fifteen cents!" he called out in Teochew.

Dried noodles cost an extra five cents due to the extra chilli *sambal* paste and tomato sauce that was used. The taste and success of a *Mee Pok Tah* hinges largely on the quality of this sauce. Ah Seng's *Mee Pok Tah, Dried Wheat Noodles,* were renowned. It was rumoured that as a young boy himself, he had clapped bamboo clackers for Tang Joon Teo, founder of *Lau Dai Hua Noodles* and had picked up the secrets of Mr Tang's *Teochew Minced Pork Mee Pok Tah*. Mr Tang had plied his trade at the Hill Street hawker centre. In those days, the centre was simply a collection of itinerant hawkers who came together with their mobile stalls. They were not housed in any building and they all sat outdoors. Hill Street was not far from the Singapore River, so the food centre had the benefit of a riverside ambience. A story that went round was that Mr Tang was saved by the popularity of his noodles. Apparently during the Japanese occupation, many of Mr Tang's customers were Japanese officers who loved his noodles. Mr Tang had been randomly selected to be executed by the *Kempetai*, the Japanese Military Police. Luckily before the execution could take place, one of the officers who patronised his stall recognised him and managed to get a reprieve for him.

Ah Seng parked his cart under the shade of a sprawling *banyan* tree so that his customers were out of the glare and burn of the tropical sun.

Like Pavlov's dog, conditioned to react to a bell ringing, I salivated every time I heard the *tik-tok, tik-tok*. Chinese village children, as well as Peranakan ones like myself, ran out of our houses just to see him. Eyes opened wide at the sight of steam rising from his aluminium cauldron. Our lips smacked at its delicious aroma of stewed pork bones. The Malay children would watch from afar; for them, the smell of pork was anathema. Most times my brothers and I watched with envy as customers lined up to be served, our stomachs gurgling and grumbling.

"Not today. Maybe tomorrow," Mak said, regret in her voice.

Then I would stick my thumb in my mouth and suck on it instead.

The sights and sounds of a rural community certainly differed from those of a city. Though our kampong was hardly more than ten miles away from *High Street*, which was the heart of town, we were an emotional ocean apart. The High Street was the first proper road in Singapore, having been the first to be sealed with tarmac. In 1821, the British cleared the thick undergrowth from the foothills of Fort Canning right down to the sea, which used to be on the edge of the Singapore Cricket Club until the land reclamation of 1890. The seafront promenade called the Esplanade was created with Victorian-style concrete balustrades similar to those found in the seaside town of Brighton in East Sussex, England; except that here the walk-way was lined with fan-palm trees which swayed languidly in the incoming sea-breeze. The main feature of the Esplanade Park was a beautiful fountain, its water cascading down and cooling those standing around it. The promenade was where the British and locals loved to walk in the balmy evenings to take in the sea air. In Malay, we called this *makan angin*, literally *to eat (the) wind*. When Queen Elizabeth ascended the British throne in 1953, it was renamed *Queen Elizabeth Walk* in her honour.

The High Street was the shopping paradise for the rich. It was the trading ground for Northern Indian settlers who ran their retail businesses and small department stores in the two-storey shophouses, supplying French lace to the expatriates, as well as clothes, fabrics and jewellery. The Europeans could have their suits and dresses tailored in silk and linen. Of course there was the *Metro*, a local department store. Across the Singapore River at Raffles Place was *Robinson's*, a luxury department store which first opened its doors in 1858.

"I'll treat you to a trip to town for your birthday," my father said to Mak.

My mother's birthday, like mine, was in March. Hers was on the 3rd and mine was on the 18th. Mak was about to turn forty-one, yet she looked as slim and beautiful as ever, always elegant in her *sarong kebaya*. It was rare for Ah Tetia to make any romantic gestures, so when he did, it meant he was amorous. There were only two beds in our attap-hut, one which he slept in with my elder brothers and the other was for my mother, who slept with us girls. How he managed to assuage his desire thereby spawning more children was a mystery to me. (Two sisters and one brother were born after me.)

"Oh, that will be so lovely! Can I bring Ah Phine? It's also going to be her birthday."

"Ya, why not? She has brought me good luck. I had a pay rise the day she was born and we were able to move from that wretched hut to this place. At least we don't have to smell the *jambans* anymore."

My parents' first home in *Kampong Potong Pasir* was a small wooden cubicle with a mud-packed floor. They slept on a platform bed with the boys. The worst thing was its location right in front of the communal outhouses. They could not escape the sickening stench when the buckets filled up and the wind blew in their direction. Having meals when the smell was strong made it hard for them to swallow their food. But we still used the same outhouses, as they were the only ones available in the village, just two cubicles for so many in the village! They were the bane of my young life. I loathed their vile odour. Mosquitoes, cockroaches, lizards, centipedes and rats treated the place as their food source and recreational ground. So, when I had to answer the call of nature, I trembled with fear that the cockroaches might run over my feet or that the rats might nip my exposed bare bottom. These childhood fears became my nightmares. My mother was very understanding and would always wait for me outside the wooden cubicles in case I needed her. At night, she permitted me to use the chamber-pot so that I did not have to face the black, bristly rats in the dark.

"One day all this will pass," she tried to assure me.

Her optimism about a better existence was my beacon of hope.

"The boys can look after each other," my father said. "You can leave Agatha with the neighbour. We'll walk down the High Street for you to look into the shops, maybe even *Robinson's*. Then we'll walk down the Esplanade and eat *satay* on Beach Road."

Agatha was three; two years younger than I was.

I was so excited. Going into town was very special indeed. For us it was almost like going to a foreign country. Window-shopping was the best we could afford.

Watching my mother getting ready to go on an outing was a treat in itself. She selected a different kind of *kebaya* than the type she wore at home to do housework, normally fastened with safety pins. She chose one made of voile with pretty peonies and a phoenix that she had embroidered by hand. The material was see-through, so she wore a cotton chemise underneath. This was the main difference between a Peranakan *kebaya* and a Malay one. The Malays tended to match their *kebaya* in the same *batik* material as their sarong. Also the front panels of their *kebaya* were cut horizontally across the hip rather than tapered like the Peranakan *kebaya*.

Kebayas originated as an Arabic long tunic then evolved into its present shape and length, moulding itself around the curves of the female body. The Peranakans' design was influenced by the Dutch in Malacca and Indonesia who added lace and embroidery to the *kebaya*. Dutch women had adapted their own long blouse to make it into an embroidered cotton tunic to suit the sweltering tropical climate of South East Asia. Malacca was a sea-port, which was an important stopover from ships from the West. The West also came to the East for tea, opium and spices like nutmeg and cloves. So it was inevitable that the Western powers fought to dominate it and to control the Straits of Malacca. First it was the Portuguese, then the Dutch, then the British. The Dutch held control in Malacca for one hundred and eighty four years, from 1641 to 1825.

Mak rummaged amongst her sarongs to retrieve her precious gold *kerosang*, a three-pin brooch linked by a fine chain to hold the *kebaya* together.

"This is the only thing I've got left from my previous life," she said without rancour. She meant her life in Malacca with her rich parents. Tragedy had claimed my grandfather, and grandmother had fled to Singapore with her children. "I hope to save it for your wedding one day."

But it was not to be. The heirlooms I received from my mother were of a different, more lasting kind.

I helped Mak comb her long black hair and she tied it into a bun. I helped her thread the creamy *bunga melor* buds, and she tied these around her *sanggul*. The natural perfume of the flowers wafted up as she glided past. She powdered her face with *bedak sejok*, then pinched her cheeks to redden them. It was a delightful transformation, from ordinary housewife to film-star glamour.

"You want to wear something nice as well?" she asked me.

Of course I could not go into town in my home-made shorts! Kampong kids were wild. At my age, I was permitted to run around without wearing any footwear or top. I was flat-chested and brown and could pass for a boy. Since my long hair was snipped off due to the infestation of *kutu*, I definitely looked like a boy.

"How about your Chinese New Year dress? The one I sewed with the full-gathered skirt and fabric rosette."

I hated it. Mak had sewn a can-can petticoat to flounce up the skirt and its material made me hot and sweaty.

"Do I have to wear shoes?"

My feet were used to being uncased by shoes and free so my toes had spread wide and were like a chimpanzee's feet. I could pick things up quite easily with my toes, which were as agile as my fingers. I could climb trees like a young chimp and if challenged, could even swing upside down from branches. There was a cherry tree in the sandy forecourt of the village shophouses and I climbed it often to pick the cherries. I had feet like a monkey's, no wonder my father kept saying that there would be no marriage prospects for me. If I had lived in China, they would definitely have bound my feet! Dainty feet were synonymous with beauty. (This could only be proclaimed by a man!) Mine were far from dainty. I used to be able to hold a piece of chalk with my toes and draw with it! This meant that trying to fit my feet into tight shoes was excruciating.

"You certainly can't go into town barefoot!"

It was a case of enduring the pain or not going into town. So I force-squeezed my feet into my narrow Chinese New Year shoes, which were tight black pumps. They hurt. I would have preferred to wear what my mother was wearing – *kasut manek*, the traditional Peranakan sandals with glass bead panels which she sewed herself. We spent our evenings embroidering or sewing *manek*. Mak used an old-fashioned wooden frame to hold the material for her bead-work. But sewing by candle-light for years took its toll on hers as well as my eyesight. The *manek*-shoes were her going-out footwear as she normally wore *char kiak* or wooden clogs when she went about in the village. The Malays called the wooden sandals *terompah*. In this instance, Peranakans used the Chinese and Malay term interchangeably. Most times, if we used a Peranakan or a Malay term for something, it meant we may not know the Chinese equivalent. I never understood why this was so.

My father wore a plain white shirt with his trousers. He never wore his *sarong* outside our kampong. Just as we were about to leave, his friend Ah Gu came rushing into our attap hut.

The names people give their children! *Gu* is a cow in Hokkien. Fancy calling your child *That Cow*! Ah Gu was a neighbour who became my father's companion in the evenings. They usually sat outdoors after sunset, drinking their favourite tipple, a pint of Guinness, whilst they discussed politics.

"Have you heard?" Ah Gu said excitedly to my father in Teochew. "There's going to be a rally at Kallang Airport on March 18. Chief Minister David Marshall is going to address the people about our country's self-rule. Shall we go together? There's a campaign right now to collect signatures of people who want independence. I'm signing. Will you? I think it's right that the chief minister is pushing for us to manage our own internal security..."

"Ah Phine will be five on that day," My father said. "Of course I will sign the petition for independence and go with you. Just because I'm earning a living in an English company and have good bosses doesn't mean I want to be under their rule forever."

"Independence is the only way to go now. You know I respect Chief Minister David Marshall a great deal. He's trying to resolve this issue about the Chinese-educated. People like me." Ah Gu said. "The colonial government doesn't recognise our education. Our qualification can't get us into university here. He sounds a clarion call of hope for us..."

"Yes, I know it's tough for Chinese-educated people like you. But the problem is not so straightforward, because of the Chinese schools' involvement with the communists..."

"Not all Chinese-educated people are pro-communist, you know," Ah Gu said in an offended tone.

"I know. I know. Look. We'll talk another time. I'm taking my wife and daughter out to town."

The rally that Ah Gu was talking about was to take place at the Old Kallang Airport. Up until a year earlier, it had been

Singapore's civil airport. Though there had been air-strips on the island, they were mainly built for military purposes, but the first commercial aeroplanes flew out of Kallang Airport.

In 1931, Governor Sir Cecil Clementi had said, "I expect to see Singapore become one of the largest and most important airports of the world. It is, therefore, essential that we should have here, close to the heart of the town, an aerodrome which is equally suitable for landing planes and sea planes; and the best site, beyond all question, is the Kallang Basin."

The mangrove swamps surrounding the basin were filled and land was reclaimed from the sea. Kallang Airport was born and officially opened on 12 June 1937 by the British Governor at that time, Sir Shenton Thomas. The terminal building and hangar were beautifully designed in art deco style, similar to the design of the oldest civil airfield in England, Shoreham Airport in West Sussex. It had a grassy landing zone and a slipway for seaplanes. For many years, Kallang Airport was considered the "finest airport in the British Empire."

A week after the airport opened, a historic event took place. World famous female aviator, Amelia Earhart, flew in from Bangkok on her second attempt to fly around the world. She was accompanied by her navigator, Frederick Noonan, and they were on their way to Bandung. Her aeroplane, the Lockheed Electra 10E landed at Kallang Airport, which she called "an aviation miracle of the East". Sadly, it was just a few weeks after this, on 2 July 1937, that she disappeared. She was last heard from about 100 miles from the tiny Pacific atoll, Howland Island.

With the opening of Paya Lebar Airport in August 1955, the historic Kallang Airport also disappeared as such, for its operations as an airport ceased and it became a centre for the Singapore Youth Sports Council. This was where the David Marshall rally was to be held.

It felt like a long walk from our house through the dusty, pot-holed village road to Upper Serangoon Road. The sun was beating down on us and my Chinese New Year dress with its can-can petticoats irritated my skin. My shoes were having a jolly time biting my feet. If it were not for the anticipation of seeing the *High Street* and all its shops, I would have preferred to be topless and without shoes and to stay at home. I was such a peasant! My parents and I walked past the fish ponds where the Chinese men were shouting out in a kind of musical rhythm as they pulled up their nets. The bulging nets were poised in the air for several minutes, heads of fish poking through the nets, their round eyes appealing for last minute reprieve. But none came, and their mouths opened and shut, opened and shut in silent screams.

We boarded a trolley-bus to town, its thick overhead cables slithering like air-borne snakes, forming a network with other snakes at the junctions of roads. Every now and then the bell went *ping!* And the bus would shudder to a stop and some people would alight hastily whilst others boarded. I was delighted by this sound and waited in anticipation for it to happen next. *Ping! Ping! Ping!*

"Watch for this, watch for this," Mak said to me. "There's Tekka market where we go to get special things when Ah Tetia has his bonus. And soon we will go across the big Rochor Canal. It's like a river."

Mak hoisted me up so that I was off my bottom and she placed me onto my knees on the bus seat so that I could peer out of the window. Indeed, as the bus clambered across the stone bridge, I could see the water flowing. It was a strange river to me, not as wide as our Kallang River in the village and it did not have muddy or moist banks either. Through the open windows of the bus, the sounds of the city were so different from the sounds in our kampong, clamouring to be heard, exciting yet daunting.

We passed my uncle's home in Petain Road where he lived with his wife and family and my grandmother, Lao Ee. Their apartment was in a four-storey block. For me any building made of brick or concrete seemed wealthy compared with the attap-roofed huts which in our kampong were made of rough planks of wood, crudely painted with *kapor*, limestone; so badly constructed on the cheap that there were gaps in the walls where you could peep into your neighbour's house. A Chinese hawker woman wearing her *samfoo*, trouser-suit, carrying two baskets slung on a pole on her shoulders, was at the foot of the block of flats calling out, "*Ang Ku Kuih, Ang Ku Kuih.*"

The dessert she was selling was made from glutinous flour stuffed with softened yellow mung beans. The glutinous paste was coloured red and pressed into a turtle-shaped mould, hence giving it its eponymous name, *ang ku*, which was Hokkien for *Red Turtle*. Because of its vibrant colour and the symbolic meaning of the turtle, which stood for prosperity and longevity, this cake was served at auspicious Chinese ceremonies like weddings and Chinese New Year. The sweetened mung bean paste was designed to bring sweetness into one's life. The Chinese were very concerned with symbols and so Peranakans too adopted the *ang ku kuih* as their own, as well as the love of symbols and meanings. Not adhering to certain symbols or customs was taboo, which made Peranakans very *pantang*, the Malay word for *superstitious*.

Adults and children rushed to their balconies when they heard the hawker-woman's cry. A young girl shouted out from the second storey to catch her attention. The hawker put her baskets down and looked up. They had a brief discussion, presumably on what the young girl wanted to purchase. Then the young girl placed some coins in a small rattan basket and lowered it with a rope in the same way that we lowered a pail into the well. The hawker woman pulled down the basket, took the coins, then placed the *ang ku kuih* in the basket and the young girl drew it up towards her. I had never seen anything like it before as we all lived on the ground floor in the kampong so did not have a need for this system. The contrast of city to village was fascinating.

At *Dhoby Ghaut*, an area between Selegie and Bras Basah Roads, the small wood of trees was strung out with flags of washing flapping in the wind. I knew that *dhoby* was the Hindi word for laundryman, since many of the laundry-men were Indians. People must be rich to have someone else do their laundry for them, I thought.

"Look, Ah Phine," Ah Tetia called out. "That's the Cathay Building, the tallest building in Singapore."

The four-storey building was imposing. It was completely made out of concrete, not a piece of wood or attap in sight.

I thought to myself, "I bet they have flush toilets like my rich cousins."

At the junction of Bras Basah Road, a traffic policeman in his khaki shirt and shorts, wearing a pith helmet, waved his arms about in order to direct traffic.

"*Bras Basah* is a corruption of the Malay words *beras basah*, wet rice," my father said to Mak. "There's a Malay legend that it was named after the incident when a barge on the Singapore River carrying sacks of rice had overturned, causing the wet rice to spill onto this area."

My mother was impressed.

Town was a magical land of robust buildings and landscaped gardens, with colourful orchids, *bunga raya* hibiscus and bougainvillea. The roads were tarmacked and there were street lamps. I imagined that when the electricity ran through the wires, the lamps must light up with joy. At nights, our *lorongs* in the village were shrouded in darkness, instilling in the children a fear of ghouls and *Pontianak*, the legendary Malay female vampire and spirit-familiars called *polong*. Our attap roofs were rigged with cactus plants so that their thorns would snag at the long hair of pontianaks and *polongs* when they levitated and flew over our houses, according to popular belief.

There were variations as to how the *Pontianak* came about. There was actually a village in *Pulau Pemanggil*, near Mersing, which was named after her. People said she resurfaced after her death to take revenge for her death. Some said she was killed. Some said she died in child-birth. Some said she lived in banana trees, others said she lived in the *chempaka* trees. Some said she had long hair and long fingernails and loved fish. Some said she loved to devour new born babies. Others even said she loved to suck the blood of men. But all agreed that she took on the form of a beautiful woman until she found her victim, before showing her ugly wizened self. A *polong*, on the other hand was said to be a personal spirit kept by someone who indulged in black-magic.

Ping! I was startled by the sudden sound as my thoughts had strayed to the Pontianak and polong. My father had pressed the bell.

"We're there. It's time for us to get off."

I practically leapt off the last step of the bus, leaving all thoughts of evil spirits behind. Surely neither a Pontianak nor a polong could survive in the city, with all its electric lights?

High Street was a different country! The grand Adelphi Hotel stood at the corner like some great matriarch looking down at the more humble shophouses and five-foot ways. Saint Andrew's Cathedral, regal and imposing, sat in a verdant landscape of lawn and trees. There was such a burst of colour and light as we strayed into various shops. My mother held my hand tightly and when she was fingering a bolt of fabric, she pressed me close to her sarong. I stood amongst a thicket of legs, afraid to get separated from my parents. I could hear my mother's sighs of contentment and I knew she was happy even though she did not buy anything. And I knew my father was happy too because for the first time, I saw him holding Mak's hand. When we peered at the elaborately dressed windows of the shops, they stood pressed hip to hip. Glass window-panes were a novelty to us, as the windows in our village were wooden shutters.

"Wait till you see the toys at Robinson's," Ah Tetia said to me.

My heart pounded in anticipation. I could feel my feet squashed to death in my shoes but I gallantly walked without whingeing because I wanted to see what toys from a store looked like when they were new. Any store-bought toy I had so far, came from the dustbins of the English children from *Atas Bukit*, at the top of the hill above our village. Most of the time, we had to make our own.

My father did not feel comfortable in taking us into *Robinson's* itself, as its customers were all richly dressed and were mostly *angmoh*, Europeans. We just gazed in awe at its magnificently dressed windows resplendent with wonderful things. We pressed our noses so close that our breath steamed up the glass panes. My mother oohed-and-ahhed over the beautiful crockery and home items and I held my breath at the sight of gorgeous dolls with blonde hair and blue eyes, large cuddly teddy bears with fur, a toy train whizzing along its tracks set in the verdant English countryside. I noticed that the uniformed doorman was watching us critically, perhaps wondering whether to tell us to move on. This subtle disapproval of our circumstance was something I became more aware of as I grew older. Poor people were like a bad smell to the rich or a disease that they might catch.

"Come on," my father said, conscious of the doorman's looks. "Let us walk through *Change Alley* and then we will go and see the fountain at the Esplanade."

It was going to be a fair walk from Raffles Place to the Esplanade so I asked, "Can I take my shoes off?"

"No!" my father said sharply. "Do you want people to regard you as *ulu*?"

Ulu was Malay and Peranakan for a place that was remote, but it also referred to someone who acted naïve, at worst stupid, like an ignorant country bumpkin. A similar expression in Hokkien was *Sua Ku, Mountain Turtle*. It was the ultimate insult. Though he did not show it earlier, my father's feelings must have been rankled by the doorman's attitude, causing him to lash out at me.

Fortunately Ah Tetia's dark mood evaporated as quickly as it had appeared. He held my hand tightly as we pushed through crowds at *Change Alley*, which was a street bazaar that had all sorts of peddlers with colourful crafts, saris and costume jewellery. There were many Indian Money Changers, which must have given the street its name. My father walked us down Cavenagh Bridge and down to the seafront Esplanade Park. As he worked in an English company, he was a fount of information about the English and the buildings they re-created here in Singapore to reflect their own. Also he loved to show off to Mak, pointing out this and that to us – places like the Fullerton Building, which was the city's main post office. At the park, he stopped by a magnificent tiered water-fountain in Wedgwood Blue, decorated with statues of nymphs and cherubs, water spouting out from the mouth of a gargoyle. The sound of cascading water was lovely. My father gesticulated with his hand.

"This is Tan Kim Seng Fountain."

"Who is Tan Kim Seng?" Mak asked.

"He was a Peranakan philanthropist who donated $13,000 in 1857 towards building Singapore's first public waterworks so that people could get fresh water in town. Of course it has not been piped down for us to use in the villages yet, but one day it will. That's what our local politicians are promising us anyway."

"It will be a small miracle for us to be able to turn on a tap in our houses and have water flow out of it. We won't have to cope with drawing water out of a well, nor suffer when the rains don't come and the well dries up. Our lives won't be dictated too much by the weather." Mak said with a sigh.

Despite his earlier retort, my father lifted me up and helped me stretch out my arm so that I could reach out to wet my hand under the falling water. It was rare to share moments of tenderness with my father or have such close physical contact with him, so my experience was intense. It was a treasure that I saved as a golden nugget of memory. Things like my mother's *kerosang* or *sireh* box could be preserved as heirlooms but the best heirlooms I saved were memories of my family.

"These statues all look so *angmoh*," Mak said. "Their features are not Asian at all. The fountain must have been built by someone English."

"You're so perceptive. You make observations like no one I know."

My father *was* in an amorous mood. Otherwise he would not have complimented my mother. I had never heard him say anything complimentary to her before. The perfume from the flowers in her hair must be going to his head. Or maybe her sexy see-through *kebaya* had something to do with it. Suddenly Mak became all coy, smiling and lowering her head.

"The person who built it was Scottish. Scots. Whatever," he continued. "His name was Andrew Handyside. He was born in Edinburgh in Scotland. He was famous for making ornate bridges, railway stations, market halls and fountains all over the world. This fountain was made in Derby, England, at his Duke Street Iron Foundry. It was initially installed at Fullerton Square in 1882 but was moved here in 1925."

Other people standing near the fountain heard my father speak and they turned to look at him, their faces reflecting that they were impressed by his wealth of knowledge. They turned back to examine the fountain with new eyes.

"You're so clever," my mother whispered, returning his compliment. They were definitely *in the mood* that day. "I don't know how you can know and remember all these things. Working at *William Jacks* has been good for you."

William Jacks was an English general merchant company that sold things like weighing scales. The company had its premises in Bukit Timah. My father was their bill-collector. But I was not interested in my parents' conversation. I was too preoccupied running round the fountain and playing with the water to see them exchange knowing glances. They must have been pleased to have uninterrupted moments to themselves as I busied myself with the fountain and skipping up and down the park. I was no longer tormented by my tight shoes, I was so happy.

"Are you hungry yet?" Ah Tetia asked.

"*Ya-lah!*" I cried out enthusiastically.

Talk of food always had the power to capture my attention. I was already having such a wonderful day and to have something to eat as well would crown the day. We traversed the length of *Queen Elizabeth Walk*, the breeze ruffling my hair. Cautiously, my parents let me stand between the stone balustrades to look down at the waves lapping against the sea-wall. I felt a huge unnamed yearning when I saw the sea spread out in ripples before me, the horizon a distance away, the fluffy clouds in the late afternoon sky. I would have loved to know where in the world the waves had been. The smell of salt in the air lifted my spirit.

So too did the smell of satay roasting outdoors on their burning charcoal beds.

"This is *Satay Club*," my father announced when we got to Beach Road. "Well, it's not actually a club but the hawkers are all satay sellers and they group here, so it's like a club."

Rows and rows of Malay men squatted beside their stalls, roasting the wooden skewers of marinated mutton, beef and chicken over burning coals. Some roasted the intestines of cows as well, called *babat* in Malay. The hawkers had come from afar, from the many kampongs, carrying their wooden stalls on sturdy rattan poles so their bare brown arms were sinewy and muscled. Like Ah Seng, they even carried low stools for their customers to sit on. The aroma of the *satay* was mouth-watering. Each time a *satay*-man spread oil on the satay, there was a lively eruption of orange and blue flames. As the brush he used to oil the satay was made from sheaves of *pandan*-leaves tied together, its contact with the raw flames scorched the leaves and sent the delicious fragrance of aromatic *screw pine leaves* into the air. He fanned the flames with his palm-fan, making the flames grow larger, dancing wildly.

"Let's sit here," my father said, drawing a low stool for Mak to sit on.

He acted very gentlemanly that day. My father ordered lavishly. He was giving my mother and me a specially good treat. I was in my element, dipping the barbecued satay and squares of *ketupat*, rice-cakes, in the spicy, crunchy peanut sauce. I did not care that we were sitting by the roadside, the fumes from the buses and cars mingling with the smoke from the fire, the sound of their engines loud in our ears. I was strangely unperturbed that a few yards away the rats were poking their heads out of the monsoon drain, taking their chances by scuttling amongst peoples' feet to steal a morsel or two. As the day darkened, the flames from the barbecue pits seemed to roar with more gusto, their bright colours brightening up the evening.

That night my feet were red and sore and they throbbed. But I was so exhausted from the day's activities that as soon as my head touched the pillow, I started to drift off. I was vaguely aware that in the darkness, my father had made his way into my mother's bed.

My mother woke me up on March 18 with the traditional Peranakan birthday snack of sweetened *mee sua* with a boiled egg in it. She had got up early to prepare it. As I took the first mouthful, I nearly spat it out as it was so sickly-sweet.

"You have to eat it all if you want to have a better life!" Mak said. "The sugar is to bring sweetness and good fortune. Hopefully our circumstances will change and your future will be brighter and never again will you have to live in the conditions we have here. The boiled egg is a symbol of fertility so that you will have children to take care of you in your old age. The long strands of noodles are for your long life."

Who would dare to thwart the God of Good Fortune when put like that? So I forced myself to eat the gooey *mee sua*. Then Mak gave me an *ang-pow*, a red packet with some money in it, the red colour symbolising good luck, and the money for prosperity. There was 80 cents in it, the number eight being another Chinese lucky symbol. Eighty cents was a lot of money for me. It could buy me eight bowls of Ah Seng's *mee tng*. Not that I'd spend it all on one thing.

"Can I use it to buy myself a ribbon, Mak?"

"Okay. Don't spend more than ten cents though."

So off I went to our village shops; some of them were just wooden lean-tos. Mak Boyan selling her delicious *bee-hoon* and *Ikan bakar*, Samy with his ice-ball, Ah Sim with her boiling cauldron of turtle eggs, which we ate by sucking it out through a hole punched into its end. *Kakar* at the corner was an Indian shop which sold a plethora of interesting things. The moment one entered the shop, one could smell the fragrant spices piled up in gunny sacks. He sold rice, lentils and other cooking ingredients as well as useful household items like brooms and batteries. Kakar's shop was like an Aladdin's cave. I knew he also sold wheels of brightly coloured ribbons.

"It's my birthday and I have 10 cents to buy a ribbon," I announced to Kakar proudly, showing him the money in my palm.

"How old are you today then?"

"Five," I said, trying to sound grown-up.

"What a lucky girl you are. Which colour would you like?"

He reached out and brought down the box of ribbons for me to select. There was a whole rainbow of colours and it was so difficult for me to choose. Finally I chose yellow.

"Normally for ten cents, I give you ribbon in twelve inches," Kakar said in the way Indians talked. "But since it's your birthday, I will give you extra."

I was so delighted that I skipped all the way home. I would have recalled that day with joy if not for the disaster that followed.

Several of the villagers were going to the All-Party Merdeka Rally at the Old Kallang Airport. People were keen to attend to find out how their lives could be improved. Ah Gu came for my father and they left together with Samad, Abu's father and our neighbour Gopal. A six-member British Parliamentary delegation from London had arrived and the rally was organised to show the British that Singapore wanted independence; *merdeka* in Malay. Twenty five thousand people attended the rally. These were mostly men.

We heard all about it when our villagers came home. Several were injured, some maimed. Wives and mothers, including Mak, rushed out of homes to greet them, and found them hobbling, their faces bruised, arms bloody.

"What happened?" Everybody asked at once.

"There were thousands of people..." Samad said.

"Yes, pushing and shoving," said Ah Gu.

"Carrying placards and banners that asked for *merdeka*," Ah Tetia said.

"Then Chief Minister David Marshall invited us to go on the stage to raise our arms and shout *merdeka*. We thought it was a good idea so we went up," said Gopal. "There were so many people jostling up there with us on the stage. Then there was a creaking sound, the stage moved and then collapsed. People were piled on top of each other, squashed like sardines..."

"It was chaos after that..." Samad said.

"Luckily we got out alive," Ah Tetia said.

"Luckily the Chief Minister was not hurt either. He was whisked away by security men..." said Ah Gu

"Was anyone killed?" The villagers asked.

"We don't know. We just tried to escape." Gopal said. "There were ambulances, fire-engines and police."

The Straits Times reported the next day that fifty people, including twenty policemen, were seriously injured. Sadly the incident did not help Chief Minister David Marshall's reputation with the visiting British Members of Parliament (MPs). They doubted the Marshall government's ability to control internal security. Disillusioned that he had failed in his attempt to get self-government, David Marshall resigned and Lim Yew Hock succeeded him as Chief Minister on June 8. It was now up to. Lim Yew Hock to sound the clarion call of hope for the people.

"Ah Gu and I are going to the opening of the new *Merdeka Bridge*. It's not any old bridge but is a symbol of our country's aspiration for independence. Would you believe that the word *merdeka* was actually suggested by an *angmoh*, Mr Francis Thomas, who used to be a teacher at Saint Andrew's School but is now

Minister of Communications and Works? The ceremony will be on August 18. Do you want to come?" Ah Tetia asked my mother. "It's an important occasion for Singapore. The new bridge is constructed over the Kallang Basin to link the two stretches of the new *Nicoll Highway* so that we can get from the City to the East Coast more easily."

Mak was pregnant again. It was a regular situation for her every other year. But this time, it was the consequence of the March birthday treat. The baby was due in December. She accommodated her growing belly by letting out her sarong.

"I'm already five months now. Better not." Mak said.

"I'll take Ah Phine. There's bound to be fireworks and other displays. She'll love it."

I was so glad he took me. The bridge was magnificent. It was 2,000 feet long and 65 feet wide. Thousands of people turned up to celebrate. My father carried me to squeeze past the huge crowd. It was late afternoon, so the sun was not too strong and the shadows from the Casuarina trees with their fine needles were already falling upon us. The pageant would end at sunset, just in time for the fireworks display. Ah Tetia lifted me onto his shoulders so that I could see. It was another of our intimate moments for me to treasure.

At the entrance to the bridge stood a tall monolith with two lions back to back against it. The stone lion, designed by Italian artist Rodolfo Nolli, was named the 'Merdeka Lion'. We did not have independence yet but it was named in the *hope and anticipation* of independence. Everyone felt a strong sense of joy and pride. There was a promise of hope in the air – that one day, we would truly be free to rule our own country. It was the first stirrings of a feeling that would grow into a cohesive force that would form our future nation. All the ethnic communities contributed something for the major event. The Chinese staged their usual dragon dance and fired thousands of fire-crackers, their exploding sound like a stampede of cows' hooves; their splintered paper raining down over our heads in a shower of red. The Malays, dressed in traditional outfits, presented a *koleh* procession, rowing their narrow boats or *koleh* across Kallang Basin. But the most memorable for me was the Indian community's contribution. They had chartered a small aircraft whose engine droned as it flew over the river mouth. The small plane swooped over the newly inaugurated Merdeka Bridge and then in a breathtaking display, the people in the plane threw out rose petals which spiralled downwards like confetti all over the bridge and all over us. It was truly spectacular.

A hawker peddling his wares, 1950s.

Author's Parents' wedding
picture, 1932. Mak was 17
and Ah Tetia was 20 when the
photo was taken.

Author's parents in the yard of 315-P in Kampong Potong Pasir.
Mak was 45 while Ah Tetia was 48.

An attap house on stilts at the Kallang basin, 1950s.

Freedom From Tyranny
(1957)

TYRANNY COMES IN many shapes, colours and forms. The tyrant controls and wreaks terror amongst those he tyrannises. Its might could force people to cower, or it could rouse the community spirit and make people stick together and fight in self defence. For a few weeks, our village had been clutched by fear – a tyrant slid amongst us, killing those in his wake; and no one could catch him. Fortunately, so far he had not attempted to kill any humans. But the history of behaviour of his kind had taught us that his proclivity could change.

Beyond our kampong – clusters of wooden huts with thatched attap-roofs that were arranged around a maze of narrow *lorongs* or passageways – lay wide fields of wild grass called *lallang*. The stiff, tall grass, some taller than a child's height, had razor-sharp edges and could nick your bare flesh, drawing blood.

And yet those same fields could be inviting, swaying languorously in the breeze, as if waving to adults and calling children to venture into them. The area held a kind of allure for those who were adventurous. It was a place for catching fish and eels, even frogs, which the Chinese called *Chwee Kway*, *Water Chicken*, and loved to eat. The grassland was also a playground for the fertile imagination, where heroes and pirates brandished their swords. The Malay kids pretended to be Hang Tuah or Hang Jebat or cowboys and Red Indians, leaping over wetlands populated with blood sucking leeches, fashioning arrows from the spine of coconut leaves and bullets from cuts of thick vines. Some folks said that this was where fairies and ghosts like the *pontianak* hide. The mood of the place could change with the weather, sombre and frightening when dark, delightful when sunny. Butterflies flitted back and forth, creepers of morning glory with their purple bell-shaped flowers festooned across shrubs and trees, giving the grassland an aura of pastoral bliss.

What was more important to the villagers was that the grassland was an Aladdin's cave of food. For those with an expert eye, food could be found in its undergrowth and vegetation, in its ditches and ponds. The *assam* or tarmarind trees grew there, their brown pods hanging down invitingly. Many of our local dishes used tamarind as a sauce or base, so the pods never stayed long on the tree. Children swam in the pond for fun, or to catch fish and eels. One of the plants that grew there in wild abundance was a root vegetable, tapioca, or *ubi kayu* in Malay. My mother, *Mak*, like many of the villagers, had devised many recipes from its tuber and its leaves. Peranakans were reputed to have the knack of creating exotic dishes from the most ordinary of ingredients. And my mother was a Peranakan cook *par excellence*.

During the days when we hungered for something more than boiled rice with soya sauce, she would send my elder brothers into the grassland in search of tapioca.

"Go carefully," she would say to them. "Beware of the snakes, *huh*. Pick what you can. We will make *lemak* with the tapioca leaves. Make sure you pluck the younger shoots because the older leaves will be too fibrous to chew."

Mak's *lemak* was made with rich freshly squeezed coconut milk, ground chillies, onions, lemon grass, *buah keras* or candlenuts and the fragrant *limau perut* or lime leaves. It was a soupy kind of dish and the tapioca leaves were boiled in the spicy soup. When my father, Ah Tetia, got his Christmas bonus from the English firm where he worked, we might have the luxury of fresh prawns to add to the *lemak*. The prawns would give the gravy that special sweetness which fresh seafood had the capacity to do. We never took for granted the food that we had the good luck to eat.

Though hidden from common view, the *lallang* grassland had a thriving population of wild rodents, salamanders, frogs and snakes. Nesting birds also made the *lallang* their home and their refuge. Though they might be a source of food for some people, Mak would never permit us to kill a bird for that purpose.

"They herald the sun with their birdsong, and bring joy," she said.

When desperate, we might steal their eggs, but we would not slaughter them for meat. For I too knew the joy my mother spoke of. My heart swelled with happiness if I beheld the sight of a wild bird, a white egret with its long beak, patiently waiting to catch a fish, the kingfisher flaunting its shimmering bright colours in flight, or a long-tailed lime-parrot winging its way back and forth amongst the trees. My mother was a very special lady indeed and for a simple kampong woman she seemed to sprout all kinds of thoughtful sayings. I saved them like precious heirlooms, locked safely in my heart.

Rural folks still owned the uncanny knowledge of sourcing food and medicine from nature. They knew which plants, seed or bark to eat and to use for medicine. Except for the disgusting cod-liver oil which Ah Tetia made us take each morning, all our medicines came from nature. Our village *bomoh* or medicine man, Pak Hassan, called the wilderness his pharmacy. He was a natural homeopath. My mother too had his unique gift. Both of them worked from their intuition and sometimes they would discuss the best folk remedy for this or that ailment. A neighbour came to her once with his foot almost severed from its ankle and she bound it with crushed *dokong anak*, a herb she found in the fields.

"You'll go to prison one of these days," my father warned her. "You might kill someone with one of your concoctions. You've no education and no learning. Don't act like a doctor."

But amongst the plethora of goodness that lay in the grassland, our tyrant lay in wait. Camouflaged. Hiding. It was the python, a snake indigenous to the tropics. No one had seen him yet but the evidence of his presence lay in his wake, clusters of feathers left behind by chickens and ducks he had swallowed, a track of dried leaves and dirt pushed aside as he slithered past; *lallang* and undergrowth flattened out by his weight.

"The *Ular Sawa* is about ten-foot-long," village python-expert, Pak Osman, declared. *Ular Sawa* is the Malay term for a python. Our village was a Malay kampong as opposed to Chinese kampongs, which reared pigs. "See how wide apart the debris is here? That's the width of his body."

He used the Malay pronoun *dia-*, to describe the python. This pronoun refers to both genders, so unless heard in context, it was sometimes difficult to know if a person was referring to a male or female. *Pak* was short for *bapak* or *father*, and was used as an honorific to address older men politely. Like many of the men living in the village, Pak Osman's cinnamon brown chest was bare, and he was clad only in a check sarong. The elders of the village, all old Malay men, followed Pak Osman's fingers pointing to the ground. There, drawn into the sand and mud was a trail that suggested the python's length and his swaggering gait.

"*Ya, Allah*! Oh my God!" One of them wailed. "He seems big enough to swallow a child then."

"No doubt about it. A python can certainly swallow something the size of a goat. Its jaw is mobile and can open very wide. He has special bones that act like a hinge. When he's swallowing something large, his windpipe thrusts out like a snorkel so that he can still breathe. His skin is stretchy, that's why he is able to expand. We must warn all the villagers not to go into the grassland until he's caught. That's where he must be hiding." Pak Osman said.

"Pak Osman, how does the python kill his victim? Does he chew it to death?"

"No, *lah*! He doesn't chew it, though his teeth are curved backwards so the victim can't escape once it's within the jaws. First the python coils himself around the victim. Then he squeezes the victim, breaking its bones to deflate the bulk. When the victim exhales, the snake increases the pressure until the victim's heart stops. Then he swallows it whole."

"Ouch!" Someone exclaimed.

"We have to spring a trap," Pak Osman said. "We have to catch him when he's just eaten something big. He will then have difficulty in moving for a while until the victim gets digested. That's the time to get him. Meanwhile we have to make pitch-forks that we can use to anchor the length of his body to the ground whilst someone hacks him to pieces with a sharp *parang*."

"The python must be evil."

"No, my child," Pak Osman explained kindly to the girl who was my friend Fatima. "The python is not evil. Its nature is to survive, just as we human beings need to survive. If he stayed in his own environment and did not bother us, we wouldn't have to kill him. It is because he has encroached on our freedom that he has become a tyrant and has to be eliminated."

"So a tyrant is someone who takes away the liberty of another person?" Fatima's elder brother, Abu, asked. But Pak Osman was too preoccupied to respond.

"No one should go near the grassland until we catch the python!" The warning was issued all around the village.

"What's a python?" I asked my mother. After all, I was only six.

"It's a giant *ular*," Mak said.

"Does it mean we're not going to get any tapioca? I want some baked tapioca. I want some baked tapioca." I grumbled petulantly.

My mother made the most delicious *kuih bingka ubi*, baked tapioca. She would grate the tapioca tuber and coconut finely, then mix it with *gula Melaka*, raw palm sugar. She'd press the mixture into a pan, then bake it in her improvised oven over her charcoal stove. When cooked, the top would be a rich golden brown, and crusty, whilst the inside would be moist and crumbly. It was mouth-watering. My mother made cooking an art.

"We can go and dig up tapioca another time. But when the snake is caught, the elders will distribute the meat and I will make python steaks for you. Or we can have a barbecue or python *satay*." She said.

"Python *satay*, python *satay*," I sang.

"Don't go out at night," Pak Osman stopped by to tell every household. "The python has poor vision, so it uses its unique infra-red sense. Therefore it can navigate perfectly in the dark. That's the time it will feel safe to come into the village grounds."

"Lock your chickens properly in their coop!" Someone shouted.

There was no ceiling across the wooden rafters underneath the attap-roofs, so voices could be heard along the terrace of houses. Every time someone dropped a dish or glass on the cement floor, its clatter echoed throughout. At night, people muffled their moans and lowered their groans.

"Don't forget to lock your children in too..." Someone added.

"And your wives," a male voice said. "Or maybe not..."

Somebody guffawed in response. Then a loud smack was heard. His wife must have shut him up. It was not easy to keep secrets, living in a kampong.

Fatima and Abu came round to our house, full of excitement. Fatima was nine, a pretty girl with skin that glowed with a deep copper-tone tan. Abu, now fourteen, was the village whiz-kid at *chapteh*. They came from a family of twelve. Nearly every family in the village had more than ten children, many of them sleeping on one bed.

"Ah Phine, my father's taking us up-country!"

"Wah! Up-country to *Tanah Melayu*?"

"Yes," Fatima enthused. "Where we can see mountains and rubber plantations."

"My brother took me once to *Batu Tinggi* to see the tall waterfall."

"Oh, there're lots more waterfalls much higher than *Batu Tinggi*," she said.

My mother's family had come from that country, from Malacca on the West Coast. Peranakans were largely known as either Malacca or Penang Peranakans. As both these places and Singapore used to be called the Straits Settlements, people called us *Straits Chinese* to differentiate us from the Overseas Chinese, who kept their own culture and customs. Peranakans integrated both the Chinese and Malay cultures.

"Is your father taking you away because of the python?"

"No," Abu said. "There're lots more pythons in the jungles up there. People don't worry about them unless they attack. Bapak is taking us to visit our grandparents. They live in the big *bandar*, Kuala Lumpur."

I remembered Mak telling me about the mountains in Malaya. We spent most evenings in the light of the hurricane lamp or carbide lamp sitting on our cement floor whilst we embroidered chemises or beaded slippers to sell. She had taught me the Peranakan crafts as soon as I could thread a needle. She loved telling me stories of her previous life, which I stored carefully in the pages of my memory. Sometimes she would allow herself a treat and chew her *sireh* (betel leaves) as we worked. Her wooden *sireh* box, or *Tepak Sireh*, was a poor replica of the one she had in Malacca, made by Malaccan craftsmen when her family was rich. Each box had partitions to hold the various ingredients like the betel leaf, areca nuts and lime paste. I often watched, mesmerised by her long, slender fingers filling the leaf with the ingredients, then folding it into a tight quid and then pushing it into her cheek. When she chewed it, the combination would turn into red juice which she spat out into a small spittoon. Then she would use her red kerchief which she kept on her shoulder for the purpose of wiping her mouth.

"It's a disgusting habit," Ah Tetia used to say. "It's addictive and it will cause mouth cancer. You should give it up."

"It's tradition," she said.

But Mak did give it up eventually. Another part of her former life erased from her memory. But she still loved talking about the mountains, and she described the majesty of the Cameron Highlands and Fraser Hill to me. Both mountain ranges grew up from the spine of the Malay Peninsula and were so high that the air was extremely cool, so the English loved to holiday there.

"In the evenings, the stars dripped downward like sparkly jewels and shone with a brightness usually obscured by city lights."

Her voice was melodious.

Apparently, up in the mountains, the winds were strong, making it chilly, so people needed to put on jackets and coats, like in the picture books thrown away by the English children from *Atas Bukit*. Except that it still did not snow at Christmas like in the picture-books, though people did light log-fires to pretend that they were in their home country, so they would toast marshmallows, roast local chestnuts and put Christmas stockings up on the mantelpieces above the fireplaces.

When Mak told me things about her other life, her voice would take on a whimsical tone and her eyes would have a faraway look.

Her life of luxury and comfort in Malacca was a sharp contrast to her life here in Kampong Potong Pasir. I had a crazy dream that one day I would help her retrieve the luxury she had known.

"How will you go to *Tanah Melayu*?" I asked Abu.

It was a legitimate question as not very many people owned cars. Certainly not the majority of our villagers. Those who did, used their cars as a means of earning a living. Many in the village used their cars as 'pirate taxis', or *pawang chiar* in Teochew. Instead of the prescribed four passengers permitted in a car, the *pawang chiar* could carry as many as eight adults, squeezed against one another like sardines in a tin. This would cut down the cost of the fare for each passenger. Sometimes the *pawang chiar* was used to ferry children to school and the owner would place a wooden plank across the back seat which would allow him to carry up to twelve children!

"Oh Bapak said we will go by *kereta-api*," Abu said.

The literal translation of the Malay words, *kereta-api* is *vehicle-fire*. Presumably, the term was coined when a train was powered by coal and had a furnace. Tanjong Pagar Railway Station, located along Keppel Road, was the only railway station on our island. Opened in 1932, the station sat on reclaimed land and its foundation was reinforced with concrete pilings. The British leased the land to the Federated Malay States Railway (FMSR). The three-storey station building had an interesting mix of architectural influences, art deco in some features, neo-classical in others. The main hall had an impressive high ceiling with windows that let in natural light.

"How exciting," I said. "I would love to go on a train journey."

"Yes," said Fatima. "I'm really looking forward to it."

"Our father said that we will be able to see the new Stadium Merdeka from grandparents' home," Abu said with his usual authority. At fourteen, Abu displayed all the attributes of a leader and orator. If circumstances had been different and he had been educated, he would have gone very far in life.

"What's a stadium?" I asked stupidly.

"It's a huge place," Abu gestured, opening wide his arms. "With thousands of seats around a giant space where people can watch football or enjoy a concert. But this is a special stadium. The people of Malaya are building it to celebrate our *In-de-pen-dence*."

He used the English word, separating each syllable so that I could grasp the foreign word. My father's thinking was limited like the men of his time, so he felt that it was a waste of time and money to let girls be educated, therefore I was not permitted to go to school. So I did not know any English. Abu gleaned English words from here and there, which showed he had an agile brain.

Abu rose to his full height and stood tall, like at a political rally.

"Bapak said we've been ruled by *Orang Puteh*, (White People) for too many years. Finally we're going to rule our country ourselves! On August 31, we will be free to do so. The stadium is called Stadium Merdeka because *merdeka* means 'independence'. Freedom."

Although he spoke his father's opinions, he said it like he too was thinking of the same thing. Sometimes Abu seemed more adult than his age.

"Come on," he urged. "Make a fist of your hand and swing it upwards and say, *Merdeka! Merdeka! Merdeka!*"

What Abu said, the village children did. Fatima and I followed behind him, raising our arms and shouting *merdeka*! I just thought it was fun to follow him but really didn't have any idea of the importance or significance of our words. Soon the other kids joined us and then more kids joined us as we snaked our human-train around the yard, chanting in unison and repeating, *merdeka*! *merdeka*!

The older kampong folks looked at us amused. My father had just arrived home on his bicycle. He cycled miles each day, all the way to Bukit Timah, where his office was located, and back. He relaxed each evening with a pint of Guinness, talking about politics with Ah Gu.

"*Ya, Merdeka,*" Encik Salim said. "First Malaya, then maybe Singapore."

"Well," Ah Tetia said. "My English boss commented that the Colonial Office in London seemed to regard our new Chief Minister, Mr Lim Yew Hock, with more confidence."

"Mr David Marshall tried his best to get us internal self-government…"

Politics was men's talk in the village and since the country's first Chief Minister David Marshall's resignation in 1956, conversation had been buzzing.

Ramu, who worked as a peon at the main Post Office at Fullerton chipped in, "Wouldn't it be wonderful if Mr Lim Yew Hock's delegation to London was successful?"

"Yes indeed," Encik Salim said. "Then we will have a *Yang Di-Pertuan Negara* as head of state instead of a British governor!"

There was a new wave of hope in the country. Chief Minister Lim Yew Hock's government was making good progress. He came back to Singapore with a new Citizenship Ordinance. For the first time, people born in Singapore were classed as Singapore Citizens and not just as British.

Ah Gu told his friends the news.

"People who are born in Singapore and the Federated States of Malaya can apply for Singapore Citizenship," he announced. "Also *angmohs* who have lived here for more than two years..."

Ah Gu was a fund of political information. He loved to keep abreast of all the news and then display his knowledge to the rest of the villagers.

"Well, it will be good to be free of the British," said Pak Hassan. "But if Malaya gets her independence and we don't, it means we will be separated from the Federated States. We've been a part of them for so long..."

"Indeed," my father said. "Us Peranakans feel slightly dismayed too. We've been called *Straits Chinese* by other Chinese people because we are part of the Straits Settlements along with Malacca and Penang. If Singapore is cut off, it will be like a separation of conjoined twins. We'll be divorced from our heritage."

I had never heard my father speak in such poetic terms before. There was a great deal about my father that I did not know. Perhaps he was expressing the tentative feelings of the ordinary populace. A new era was dawning but it was not all going to be perfect.

"Okay, okay," Pak Osman said. "It's marvellous if we get our freedom from the British. But right now, my main concern is freedom from our village tyrant. We are setting the trap tonight and we need all the help we can get, *lah*."

Sivalingam was the village goat-herdsman. He lived alone with his *kambing*. He housed them underneath an attap-thatched roof supported by thick wooden posts, no wall around them, with straw and mud underfoot. During the monsoons, when heavy rain lashed at his humble dwelling and turned his floor to slippery mud, he would create a tarpaulin wall. He himself slept on a cot of rope or *charpoy* beside his animals. When you ventured near the stalls you could smell the goats' excrement and urine. Sivalingam was obviously oblivious to the smell. If you should stand close to him though, you would realise that the dank smell of his goats clung to his *dhoti* and body. He bred the goats for their milk and when the animals became too old to produce milk, he sold them as mutton to the *Tekka market* beside *Rochor Canal* in *Little India*.

Tekka was the largest wet market in the country and was a busy bazaar for fresh meat, poultry, fish, vegetables, fruits and spices. *Tek* is Hokkien for bamboo and *ka* means *by the feet* or *clump*. As clumps of bamboo grew around that area of Serangoon Road, the market was named after them. They also sold gaudy glass bangles, saris and local crafts. The building itself was magnificent, built in 1915, based loosely on the design of London's largest market, Covent Garden. All the local farmers brought their produce to *Tekka*. It was such a fascinating and exotic place that even the *angmohs* could be seen shopping here, usually with their black-and-white *amahs* or Malay drivers in tow.

Though mutton had a strong aroma, it was particularly delicious in hot curries and *dalcha*, and a local delicacy called *Sup Kambing*. Like mutton, goat's milk had a strong flavour and was considered the poor man's option to cow's milk.

"I shall provide one goat as bait," Sivalingam said, nodding his head in Indian fashion to Pak Osman. "Better to have one less goat than the python raiding my place and killing the whole herd."

He selected a goat which had recently broken its leg when it stumbled into a pot-hole. The village lanes were full of pot-holes. The goat was not producing much milk anyway and it seemed merciful to consign it to its afterlife. But still Sivalingam talked to it as if he was talking to his child, patting it, cajoling it. The village folks had often seen him muttering to his goats and thought he had gone funny after living with them for years. His goats were family to him.

That evening, with tears in his eyes, Sivalingam led the hapless goat to the stake erected by the Elders. This was in a spot not far from the grassland but in an open area so that the villagers could see all that transpired whilst waiting in the bushes with their *parangs* and pitch-forks. A carbide lamp provided the light, the naked flame, hissing and spluttering. Sivalingam reluctantly tied his goat to the stake, and as if the goat knew what was about to happen, it whined and kicked its hooves, making the dust fly.

"Shhh, shh, shhh," Sivalingam tried to placate it. "I will ask Lord Shiva to take you quickly so there'll be no pain."

After saying his farewell, Sivalingam slipped into the bushes with all the others and started a *bhakhari japa*, chanting *Om*

Namah Shivaya, Om Namah Shivaya for Shiva to assist in the goat's transition to the afterlife.

"Quiet!" Pak Osman said. "You'll scare the python off!"

So Sivalingam had to resort to the quietest of the *japa, manasik japa*. He chanted under his breath. The group waited, shivering a little as the trees and shrubs in the grassland took on spectral shapes as the moon rose. Perhaps the stories about ghosts and the *pontianak* inhabiting the grassland were true after all. The breeze picked up and brought a waft of fragrance. Everyone's flesh crawled. It was the scent of the *chempaka* flowers! The *pontianak* was a female vampire who always took on the guise of an attractive maiden. Some men longed to gaze at her legendary beauty yet were filled with dread. She was said to live in the banana tree but loved the *chempaka* flowers whose fragrance was associated with her. She was on everyone's mind. The men's imagination took flight and they almost expected her to appear out of the grassland, levitating towards them. They jumped in fright when the tall lallang suddenly parted.

But it was not the *pontianak*, it was the python.

The men gasped as the snake's head appeared, then his body. Like a blind person moving along and using his sense of hearing, the snake paused as he tried to register where his victim was located. His head swivelled here and there until it stopped in the direction of the goat, whose fidgeting had attracted him.

"I can't bear to watch this," Sivalingam said.

He left the group to go back in the direction of the village. He was glad he did not stay because he heard later that his goat bleated suddenly with fright. Then he heard the sound of his goat's thrashing hooves. The worst was happening. It broke his heart to send his goat to its demise this way.

"*Om Namah Shivaya! Om Namah Shivaya!*" He chanted loudly now to quell the sound of his furiously beating heart.

"You should have seen it, the belly of the python swollen with your goat..."

"Spare me!" shouted Sivalingam.

"Samat!" Pak Osman interrupted the man. "How can you be so uncaring? Don't upset Sivalingam with the details. Just thank him for his sacrifice that has saved the village!"

Samat offered the python steaks to Sivalingam but he would not take them.

That evening, Pak Osman organised a communal charcoal spit. By dinner time, the fire was blazing. It felt like a celebration, hurricane lamps all around to light up the place, people dressed up so the mosquitoes would not feast on their flesh. A young Malay man, Karim, the village's musical protégé, brought a guitar and started to pluck at its strings. Although uneducated, with the unenviable job of clearing the latrines and outhouses, he could play immeasurably beautiful music that moved people to joy and tears. The musical notes rose into the stillness of the evening and children clapped and danced around the fire. The atmosphere was like a *temasya*, a Malay word for a cultural evening.

Then the python steaks were brought out. The women had cleaned and prepared the meat which had been skilfully skinned, then marinated in freshly ground spices: *ketumba, jintan manis* and *kunyit*. The coriander, cumin and turmeric took away its gamey smell. Without its distinctive skin, the steaks, with a bone in the middle looked like they could be mutton chops or eel chops except that they were in larger chunks. The men grilled the steaks on the hot charcoals wrapped in banana leaves which wilted and browned and brought out a mouth-watering fragrance. Everyone in the village had a fair share.

Fatima and Abu had returned in time to share in the largesse.

"What was the stadium like?" I asked them.

"Oh it was magnificent," said Abu. "The crowd there was so inspiring. Did you know that the Federated States of Malaya will gain independence from the British on August 31? From then on, our own people will rule our country. We shall be independent. No *Orang Puteh* to tell us what to do anymore. We will be free! No more tyrants to rule over us!"

"*Oi! Budak!* Child!" Pak Osman slapped his wrist. "*Chuchi mulut dengan sabun*! Wash out your mouth with soap! Be careful with your expressions. Some words are better not said. You never know who's listening."

"But Pak Osman. Don't you think that that the *Orang Puteh* are tyrants? Don't you want Singapore to be free too?"

"I said Enough! Go and get your sister a piece of python steak."

Realising from Pak Osman's tone that he had stepped over the line, Abu quickly apologised, "*Ma'af*, Pak Osman. I'm sorry, Pak Osman!"

We were in an age when young people still deferred to their elders and showed due respect. Rude words uttered by children were punishable by washing their mouths out with soap, or more serious rudeness warranted the mouth to be stuffed with hot chilli paste, *sumbat sambal belachan*. I can testify that the latter was a fate worse than being caned with a *rotan*. I had been a naughty, outspoken girl indeed.

"*Ya, ya, ya*," Fatima said impatiently. "I'm hungry."

Abu rolled up his eyes, but he scuttled off obediently.

"What's the python steak like?" Fatima asked me, making a face.

"Oh, you don't have anything to worry about. It's very aromatic and delicious," I said. "It tastes just like fresh kampong chicken, *lah*."

Python photo, taken in the 1930s. It shows how a python gets bloated
when it swallows a big victim, like a goat in story set in the 1950s.
(Courtesy of Han Chou Yuan)

A stove that resembles the clay stove that the
author's mother, Mak, used for cooking.

Going For Gold
(1958)

IN OUR KAMPONG in Potong Pasir, we were not woken up by the harsh groans of mechanical engines or the screeching of wheels on hard tarmac. Nor were we blasted into wakefulness by loud radios. Instead, in our rural bliss, we were treated to the delightful guttural crows of a rooster or the sweet singing of the dawn chorus. Groups of starlings nesting in the tall *angsana* trees would start twittering, then stretch their wings to fly out and coast along our roofs. The *mynah* birds with their clawed feet scratched our dry attap, looking for their breakfast of beetle, lizard or centipede. The sounds would rouse us out of our sleep. In the half-light, when the first rooster crowed, it might be echoed by other cocks in the village, their harmonised music as if orchestrated by some divine conductor. It was a gentle kind of awakening, the sounds of nature lightly treading on our semi-consciousness; the sunlight softly streaming through coconut fronds – and holes in our attap roofs.

"When we lose touch with nature, our *chi* shrivels within us," my mother used to say. "It's important to breathe amongst trees and flowers; feel the wind in your hair, the sun on your skin, the sand under your toes, or smell the salt in the air. You should never be too busy to connect with nature."

Mak had a reservoir of such sayings. She was alive to life.

I could smell coffee being brewed. I loved to awake to its aroma.

It was a Sunday and my father was not working, so he was preparing breakfast, to allow Mak a few more minutes in bed. Another baby, a boy this time, had been born in the previous year, when Mak was forty-two. It was probably her sixteenth pregnancy or somewhere around that number, so she needed rest. She had so many children, she had lost count. She had a child every other year since she was married at seventeen. Conditions were dire; there was little money and nutrition was poor. When my mother shopped at the wet market, she could only afford to buy vegetable cut-offs that were meant for animal feed. Any meat she bought would be gristle or fat to flavour our soups and curries. It was no surprise then that only eight of us survived, and one was given away. There was no system of birth-control, except abstaining. But which woman dared to tell her husband to abstain?

We meant a lot of hard work for Mak, who did everything without complaint – scrubbing and washing our clothes by hand at the well, cooking on kerosene and clay stoves, cleaning with no sophisticated machines to lighten her load, clearing the smelly chamber-pot every morning. Ah Tetia was not the most domesticated of husbands and he could be demanding; and in his tortured moods, he could be violent. At other times, he demonstrated a tenderness that would melt anybody's heart. Even his features softened. It was at times like this that I understood how my mother could love him, despite his abuse.

"Wake up, Ah Phine," he said, tickling the soles of my feet. "I've got your favourite *bak ee* today to eat with *moey*, rice porridge."

His mother, my Lao Ee, made the most delicious *Peranakan* minced pork patties, little round rissoles of minced pork with chopped onions and chillies bound together with raw egg, then fried till golden brown. The taste was simply saliva-inducing, made all the more exquisite because meat was such a luxury for my family and many other families in the kampong. My father often dropped by at grandmother's place in Petain Road on his way back from Bukit Timah where he was a Bill Collector in an English firm. Petain Road was just off Serangoon Road so was not out of his way. I always thought of Lao Ee fondly, pictured her in her kebaya panjang, the handkerchief slung over one shoulder. The handkerchief was an old habit from her *sireh* chewing days, used to dab the saliva from her mouth. Like my mother, she had finally given up the traditional pastime, due to a fear of its cancer-causing propensities, and the unsavoury necessity to spit out red juice into spittoons. Her upper back was beginning to curve, so she looked as if she was constantly stooping. Lately she had adopted a shuffling gait, as if unwilling to walk briskly to her demise. Like all Peranakan women, she was a great cook. I whooped for joy whenever Ah Tetia brought home the patties she made. It was such a treat. Grandmother, who lived with her fourth son and family, was aware that our family did not get as much to eat as my uncle's family.

Eldest Brother, whom we addressed as *Ah Hiah* in Teochew, meaning Elder brother, blamed our poverty on my father's stupidity.

"It's not as if we were that poor. Father was in charge of rice-rationing in the war so he earned lots of *banana*-money." He often told our siblings in frustrated tones.

Banana money was so called because the money distributed by the Japanese conquerors had the picture of a banana tree on its notes.

"Instead of investing the money in buying a house or land, he stored it in chests underneath the bed. He never expected the British to come back. Of course, when they did return, the banana money was completely worthless!"

Arguments between my eldest brother and father often escalated into fisti-cuffs. They were both strong-willed men. In that sort of situation it was hard to see the softer side in them. But nothing is black-and-white, life has a lot of grey.

I watched my father with love for his gentleness. Ah Tetia strained the coffee with a calico-cloth bag, then poured it into an enamel coffee-pot. He stirred condensed-milk into it. By the time breakfast was served, my other siblings and Mak were also up. They took turns to bathe at the well, my eldest brother drawing up the pails of water for Mak. He had just started training to be a teacher at St. Andrew's school, the Anglican missionary school across the Kallang River from our village, where Francis Thomas used to teach before he became a Member of Parliament. Eldest Brother was an ace student in science and mathematics. If our family circumstances had been different, he could have pursued his dream of being a pilot. Instead he had to be a teacher where his training was funded, and he could start earning quickly to support the rest of us. The responsibility rested heavily on his young shoulders. In his way, he too gave me opportunities I would not have had otherwise. My mother always reminded me that we had to be grateful to those who helped us along in our life.

We sat cross-legged on our crude cement floor in the kitchen as we did not own any tables or chairs. To eat our *moey*, rice porridge, which was served in china bowls, we used chopsticks and a china spoon. This was similar to how the Chinese ate. But when we had rice, we ate it in a plate rather than a bowl; and we used our fingers to eat, like the Malays. Our Peranakan culture was a rich mix of Malay and Chinese customs and cultures. Who decided what we selected from each was a mystery to me. Ah Tetia was in his usual home attire, a checked sarong, his chest bare. He was in his late forties and was already losing his hair, but his body was rippling with muscles.

"Do you want to join me in weight-training later?" He said to two of my elder brothers light-heartedly. "Both of you look too scrawny."

Outside in the sandy yard, Ah Tetia had set up the home-built weight-lifting gym, a rough-hewn wooden bench, bar-bells hoisted across sturdy posts. Weight-lifting was his and Second Elder Brother's Sunday recreation. But he also had to keep fit because he had to cycle daily from Potong Pasir to Bukit Timah and back, which was a mean feat considering the distance. My father and brother were sometimes joined in his weight-lifting session by two younger men from the kampong, Rajah and Salleh, both of whom addressed my father as *Inche* or *Mr* Chia. My father had a kind of status in the village because he spoke some English, which was rare among us.

Our Indian neighbour, Krishnan, also spoke some English, as he worked for the City Council, though people still referred to the government body as the 'Municipal'. It was a government department dealing with roads, water and electricity, and had changed names in 1951. Krishnan stayed aloof, as he was a

Brahmin, the priestly Indian caste, and he felt he was too high-brow to socialise with the villagers. He did not even participate in the capturing of the python which had plagued the village the year before, nor joined in the barbecue afterwards. But his wife and two daughters, Devi and Lalita, did not put on any airs. I was friends with both girls, who were older than me, and like me, were uneducated. Kampong children did not have either the privilege or luxury to be educated as a matter of course, especially if they were girls. I had longed to go to school but my father had refused to let me.

"Your mother really makes such good *bak ee*," Mak said, biting into one.

My father smiled. He was really handsome when he smiled. Then, picking up one more rissole with his chopsticks, he placed it in Mak's bowl. This gesture was the height of Asian caring, and in subtler ways it was a kind of courtship ritual. A Peranakan couple on their wedding evening had to feed each other with morsels of food left out for them in the bridal chamber, before they could consummate their marriage on their elaborately decorated wedding bed. The ritual was symbolic of their nurturing each other. I hoped Ah Tetia was not getting amorous again! I did not think that Mak could survive another pregnancy.

"Eat! Eat!" Ah Tetia said.

After the breakfast things had been cleared, my father said to Mak, "Well, are you going to tell her or shall I?"

"You tell her since you've decided..."

My mother was a typical Asian woman of her time, deferring to her husband's opinion and decisions. And even if it was she who had decided, she would not let it be known publicly so that he could save face. She never argued outright. It was drummed into her that a man's ego was fragile and needed constant boosting. She was taught that he would be more agreeable when he felt himself to be lord and master in his home. It did not always work, as my father sometimes demonstrated, when his demons entered him. But still, on the whole, Peranakan girls were nurtured by their mothers and grandmothers to practise this delicate balance of appeasing their husbands, yet getting their own way. Although many Peranakan girls were not educated formally, their home education was intense. They had to learn how to cook, how to keep house and manage servants if they were wealthy; how to sew and embroider, how to play music and sing *keronchong* – and how to pleasure their husbands.

I was horrified. What were my parents going to tell me?

Maybe they were thinking of giving me away too. My heart skipped several beats at this possibility. Although it had not been discussed openly, I had understood from my brothers that one child had been given away just after the Japanese war, when Ah Tetia did not have a job. This was not unusual in rural areas; not everyone registered a birth promptly. But how it must have grieved my mother. It was the test of a mother's strength to give a child away so that he would have a better life than to keep him with her to suffer their poverty. If a boy could be given away, what lay in store for a girl like me? Ah Tetia had spelled out so many times that rice rations were wasted on girls, as we would belong to our husband's household after marriage. That was why he did not bother to educate me. He had also said, "Education poisons a woman's mind."

Though we did not have much, and life in the kampong was challenging, I did not want to be given away. I loved my mother and my family. I did not want to be separated from them. I was told that once before, when I had been six months old, my father did want to give me away. A Sikh neighbour who was childless had asked to adopt me. My father tried to persuade my mother that I should be given away. But my mother had said *No* very vehemently. Had she changed her mind now? Fear clutched at my heart and made it beat like a trapped bird in my chest.

"I've agreed to allow you to go to school. Provided that you help your mother to sell the *nonya kuih* to pay for it. No money is to be taken out of the household expenses. Understand? Maybe a bit of education will get you a job and you can look after us in our old age…"

I could not believe what I was hearing. First, I was relieved that my parents did not intend to give me away. Secondly, it was a dream come true to go to school! My mother and father had come to blows, literally, on the subject previously. I was already seven and children my age had started school the year before. It was a prospect beyond my wildest imagination. Of course my mother must have used her pillow talk to accomplish this feat. The latter was a term to describe the period when couples were in bed and chatting intimately. Usually the husband would want to exercise his conjugal rights at such times, and was willing to be more pliable and sympathetic, thus giving his woman the opportunity to ask for things he would otherwise refuse.

"Speechless, are you? What good is school going to do for you if you can't speak out?" Ah Tetia teased. "School has already started but if your mother can find a school which will take you, you can go."

Just at that moment, Rajah and Salleh turned up.

"Hey Mr Chia. Ready to carry weights or not?"

"Of course! Of course! We can all pretend we are going to compete in the British Empire Games like Mr Tan Howe Liang."

Like Second Elder brother, Rajah and Salleh had young, well-sculpted torsos. They were tall. With their dark brown bodies, they looked like heroes who had strayed from a Shaw Brothers film-set. The young men assisted my father and brother to set up the weights, chatting excitedly about the possibility of Tan Howe Liang bringing home a medal from *The Games*. Singapore's favourite sportsman and weightlifter had been born in Swatow, China and had immigrated to Singapore after the Japanese war. He had participated in the Olympic Games in Melbourne two years ago in 1956 but had not won anything. This year he was going to Cardiff, Wales, in the United Kingdom, to make another attempt. The British Empire Games were held every four years. They had been started in 1930 by a Canadian, Bobby Robinson, in Hamilton, Ontario as a way to bring the disparate peoples of the British Empire together in friendly sporting competition.

"Sure got chance *one*, this time," Salleh said with enthusiasm. "He's so determined and has trained so hard…"

"He's definitely going for gold…" Rajah said.

I was going for gold too in a different way. I was going to school! It was so precious I could hardly believe it was coming true.

My mother, who had no education and no ability to read English signs, asked many schools to take me in mid-term. She was refused by several convent schools. Eventually she met a kind principal of a Government School, who admitted me for the second term of the academic year. She was Miss De Souza of Cedar Girls Primary School, whom I considered to be my first guardian angel, for giving me a start to a new life.)

Cedar School was beyond the scenic Alkaff Gardens in Sennett Estate, a smart housing development across the road from our village. Upper Serangoon Road, a tarmac road compared to the sandy one in our village, divided us like a boundary between the poor and rich; our village was a shanty-town of wooden huts with attap roofs, whilst the houses in Sennett Estate were made of bricks and concrete and had flush toilets and electricity. The disparity was great.

"We have to go to Bras Basah Road to buy books for you," Mak said.

Two years previously, my father had taken my mother and me out for our joint birthday treat in town, since my mother and I shared the same month for our birthdays. I remembered the name Bras Basah Road because Ah Tetia had told me the story of how it had got its name. (See Chapter on *Clarion Call of Hope*). The words were supposedly a corruption of the Malay words, *beras basah*, *wet rice*. *Beras* was uncooked rice grains. As rice was a staple food in the region, the indigenous Malays had several words for rice; *padi* meaning rice on stalks in the field, *nasi* meaning cooked rice, *nasi bubur* meaning rice cooked into a gruel.

The wooden shophouses along Bras Basah road were a contrast to the concrete magnificence of the curved white facade of St. Joseph's Institution. It was a Catholic school for boys and it looked rather posh. The school faced the sprawling grounds of *The Good Shepherd*, the largest Roman Catholic cathedral in Singapore. The cathedral had a splendid spire and was a beautiful building styled after one of the churches in London, the *Church of St Martin-in-the-Fields*. It was hard to picture *The Good Shepherd* in its original state in 1832 when it had been made of wood and had an attap roof, like our kampong houses.

On the way to town, the skies had opened up and now the rain was lashing us from all sides as we disembarked from the Singapore Traction Company *(STC)* bus. Luckily my mother had the foresight to bring an umbrella, and we hugged closely underneath the waxed-paper umbrella with its wooden spokes, as we dashed to the five-foot-way for respite. Some people credited modern Singapore's British founder, Sir Stamford Raffles, with the idea of creating these open corridors under the first floor of a building to shield people from the tropical sun and the onslaught of heavy rain. Others credited Alexander Laurie Johnston for its design. He had been a prominent merchant who came to Singapore in 1852. Whoever gave birth to the concept, he was ingenious. All newly erected buildings had to provide this mode of shelter. As the width of these passage-ways was approximately five feet, they came to be called *five-foot-way*, and this came to characterise the architecture of shophouses.

"Oh, the rain is so heavy!" my mother said. "I hope your father and brothers remember to put out the pails and tins to catch the leaks."

When first weaved for our kampong roofs, *attap* was fresh, newly dried palm fronds. But continual exposure to the hot sun made them dry and brittle. Designed so that the breeze could lift them and let air into the houses to cool them, this very action sometimes caused damage to already brittle leaves. The birds foraged for food too, breaking the dry attap with their weight. As our houses did not have any ceiling, the holes would let the rain fall directly into the houses. As soon as thunder clapped, there was the usual scuttling to collect pails or kerosene tins to put under the gaps in the attap. This was what Mak was referring to.

"Don't have much money so must buy second-hand books," Mak said.

"It's okay, Mak. I don't mind. I don't mind," I said, trying to reassure her.

It was already a miracle to be going to school. I was prepared to put up with the small inconvenience of hand-me-down books which may be somewhat dog-eared, or have doodles and notes squiggled in the margins of their pages, or sentences underlined. Never had I been so filled with utter joy as on that first day of buying books. The shops, manned mostly by Indians, were an Aladdin's Cave of stationery and magazines; books piled everywhere, on tables and shelves and on the floor. Huge stacks of books towered over me and their smell was so intoxicating; especially the new books which had such a pristine and woody scent. When no one was looking, I fanned the pages of a new book in my face. Its scent became an addiction I never could be weaned from. I was a child, mesmerised, fingering all the different titles and front covers. Some of the books were so old that their pages were yellowed and curled. Pressed amongst some ancient pages were tiny silver-fish, dried and loose. Yet the books had not lost their beauty or allure for me, for within them were worlds I had not fathomed, people I had not met, places I had not been to. My mother was armed with a book-list from the principal that she could not read. Yet she wanted *me* to be able to read; persevered so that *I* could read. It was one of her greatest gifts to me.

"I want you to have a life I could not have," she said.

I am eternally indebted.

Ah Gu, my father's buddy, with whom he discussed politics, barged into our house unannounced when we were sitting in the kitchen having our dinner. His parents must have been perceptive to name him after a cow, or in his case, a bull.

"We've got it!" He said. "Lim Yew Hock's delegation to London has been successful. We are getting self-government. I heard it on the news on Rediffusion!"

"Do you want something to eat?" my father said, with typical Asian politeness but at the same time knowing that another addition to dinner would strain our meagre resources. "So Harold Macmillan had fulfilled his promise."

The British Prime Minister had stopped over in Singapore earlier in the year and when questioned on the subject of self-government, he had said, "*We will not go back on our word.*"

"No need. No need. I've eaten."

My father smiled with relief and offered him an F&N Orange drink.

"Yes," Ah Gu said. "This is a start. The British will still have control over foreign affairs and defence, but at least we can run our own country. Not quite independence, but not far from it. We will become the State of Singapore and no longer a colony."

"Looks like our whole country is going for gold..." Ah Tetia said, using the sporting metaphor.

There was a renewed air of anticipation in the country. Suddenly there was hope for a different future, one where we were ruled by our own people. Hope was a jewel for the spirit. Without hope, people would give up. In an individual way, weightlifter Tan Howe Liang too had lived in hope. He was prepared to work hard at his sport and was unafraid to dream. Someone once said, "*Without dreams, life is a winged bird that cannot fly.*" The country was in suspense during the period of the British Empire Games and it rejoiced when Tan Howe Liang finally fulfilled his dream. He came home from the Games with a Gold Medal – the first for Singapore. But he was not ready to rest on his laurels. He was not finished. He was planning to participate in the Olympics in 1960. Singapore too was not finished – it was striving for its own identity and going for gold in its nationhood.

Author's paternal grandmother, 1957.

Author's maternal grandmother, who is a
Portuguese-Peranakan, 1920s.

Music For Togetherness
(1959)

ONE OF THE most memorable delights of kampong life was its sense of community and friendliness. Neighbours talked to each other, and confided and communicated. And when the need arose, people pulled their weight together, shared and did things together. Like the time when the python reared its ugly head and the villagers got together to capture and kill it. The Malays have a wonderful expression for this heart-warming togetherness – *gotong royong*; normally translated as *mutual assistance*. It was a means of helping each other without any ulterior personal motive, but for the good of the community.

This spirit of togetherness and community was encouraged by the fact that doors in the village were often kept open and people tended to live outdoors, which meant that they knew each other and thus made this attitude possible. There was a kind of mutual trust. Perhaps also, people seemed more laid back in the kampong, not harassed by deadlines and the acquisition of material things. They did not possess the attitude that *others* should be blamed for their misfortune. Sure, the kampong folks could always do with more money and better living conditions, but they dealt with their deprivations with a kind of nobility and lived each day for the joys that the new day brought.

"Money is a currency that allows you to buy things," Mak said. "Having it does not always make you happy. True wealth is when you have equanimity and joy of spirit."

I think my mother was a living *Buddha*, if to be a *buddha* meant someone who was enlightened and acted with non-attachment. She had gone from the material comfort of her parents' home in Malacca to the dire circumstances of Kampong Potong Pasir.

Yet she performed her every task with quiet dignity, despite its abhorrent nature – emptying out the smelly chamber-pots every morning; clearing the cess-pool of slimy washing-up water; picking up the rats' droppings from our cement floor or yanking out wriggly worms from her screaming children's bottoms. Poor diet with little nutritional value and eating almost decomposed food caused intestinal worms to grow in bellies, and kampong children had to cope with the terror and torture of the live worms forcing their way out. This was what we had to live with. It was a fate worse than death to us. I cannot begin to tell you what my own experience was like – its memory is enough to give me the shudders. But we survived.

Mak never let on to the neighbours that she used to have servants to do everything for her, though her natural grace and refinement must have intimated to everybody that she was not of peasant stock. But she chose me to share her stories with, and somehow I must have stored them in the pages of my memory. (Perhaps it was my destiny to be a writer so that I could put her stories in print for her.) The only time one became aware of the possibility of her having had a better life was when the villagers got together to sing and play music. Her musical education and talents surfaced in those moments, because she had the knack of picking up almost any musical instrument to play with ease and virtuosity. In her father's grand wood-crafted house in the coastal town of Malacca, she had once played the violin and the piano. I imagined her as she was then, young and beautiful, the violin resting on her slim shoulders, her face tilted in keen concentration as she coaxed the haunting melody from the instrument. But the violin, like the piano, was eventually sold for food.

"Nonya," Karim said. "Do you want to try the ukulele today?"

People addressed Peranakan women as *nonya*. It had been suggested that the term developed from an old Portuguese word, *nhonha* which may have been a corruption of the word, *senhora*, to mean *a lady*. After all, Malacca was the birthplace of many Peranakans, therefore its culture was inevitably influenced by the Portuguese. They had occupied the city for one hundred and thirty years in the 16th century, and they had left their traces. The Dutch wrested control from them in January 1641 and ruled for the next one hundred and eighty four years. Our popular Peranakan crispy rolled crepe, *kuih belanda*, translated as *Dutch cake*, was attributed to the latter's influence.

At the day's end, when house-work and labouring were done, our village folk gathered in the sandy yard to share their day, to talk, tell stories, or sing songs. People had to entertain themselves, as technological advances had yet to reach us. The evening's activity was a rustic kind of soiree. People sat on straw mats, empty wooden crates, stools, or the horizontal lay of coconut palms. The naked dancing flames from hurricane and carbide lamps lit up the darkened evening, sending all sorts of moving shapes around. Cicadas sang their own song quite audibly and merrily. If rain was in the air, even the deep-throated frogs from the nearby river banks and ponds would contribute to the concert, singing in their baritone. Nature had its own magical symphony. But it was a dry March so no rain was imminent, therefore the frogs were sulky and silent. In the hot months, it was not unusual to come upon someone sleeping outdoors all night on their roped *charpoy* or straw mat. In the yard, banana and papaya trees stood by like straight-backed sentinels, casting tall shadows.

Karim was a cheerful and able-bodied young man, who usually initiated the *temasya* or cultural event. He loved music and used it to escape the dreariness of his occupation, that of clearing the filled-buckets from the *jambans*, or outhouses. The black oval buckets were positioned under the opening of the wooden platform of the outhouses. Rats, cockroaches, centipedes, worms, flies and mosquitoes swarmed around the open buckets. Karim's job was to drive the Municipal truck from the sewage centre at Kolam Ayer near Kallang to the villages, to pick up the buckets and swap them with clean and empty ones. People tended to joke about the long vehicle he drove, calling it a *limousine* due to its many compartments for the buckets.

"*Oi, limousine datang*! The limousine is here!" Children called out when he turned up in it.

There were no such things as rubber gloves in those days, and Karim had to handle the buckets with his bare hands. It was particularly unpleasant for him when the buckets were over-flowing and their handles smeared with faeces. After all, Malays like Peranakans eat food with their fingers! What did Karim use at the end of the day to rid himself of the smell and aura of his job? To keep his spirits up, Karim whistled as he worked, as if what he was doing was an agreeable task. Sometimes the stench was so foul, he would tie a handkerchief over his nose and mouth. Kampong folks considered men like him our unsung heroes because without them doing such menial and thankless jobs, our lives in the village would be hell. The simple, normal process of moving one's bowel would have been torment. People who lived in houses that had flush toilets could simply not comprehend our daily tribulation.

For someone whose hands handle such despicable matter, Karim's hands were unusually delicate and graceful, his fingers long and tapered. He could have been destined for better things, but life deprived him of the right opportunities, for he had no schooling. Education was not the privilege of many kampong folks. I was already eight years old and I had only just started school the previous year, after my mother persuaded my father that she would put me through school selling *nonya kuih*, Peranakan cakes, and *nasi lemak*.

In the kampongs, survival was more important than education. There was hardly enough money to eat, let alone to be schooled. So there were many like Karim, relegated to jobs beneath their true talent or stature. Yet he had such a delightful personality. He may have been poor but he was certainly wealthy according to my mother's definition, for he had equanimity and joy of spirit. Cheerfully, he handed my mother a ukulele whilst he himself opted for the guitar.

"Shall we play one of P. Ramlee's songs? How about *Getaran Jiwa?*" P. Ramlee, actor, director and singer was 1950s Singapore's local heart-throb.

"Oh yes," my mother said. "I love the lyrics and you've got the voice for it."

Karim sang the song from P. Ramlee's film *Anatara dua Darjat*, or *Between two Classes*. It was a story about a man who fell in love with a girl from the Malay royal household. The usual star-crossed lovers type of movie which brought tears to people's eyes. In the song, the couple were likened to rhythm and song. Karim brought out everyone's feelings with his emotive rendering of the words:

Tak mungkin hilang, irama dan lagu
Bagaikan kembang, sentiasa bermadu
Andai dipisah, lagu dan irama
Lemah tiada berjiwa, hampa

Never will (they) vanish, rhythm and song.
Like blossoms, (they) will linger forever.
If you separate, the song and the rhythm,
(They'll) be weak and soulless, and empty.

The lyrics carried a deeper meaning for the way we live – if we do not live in a creative way, our lives will be empty and soulless. Karim sang with feeling because music made his life meaningful. He certainly had an innate talent for music and performance. With a musical instrument in her hand, my mother too was transformed. She went from wife, mother and ordinary housewife to a talented musician in her own right. She often told me how she used to play the piano in grandfather's big bungalow by the sea in Malacca. So, seeing her with her eyes lowered as she plucked at the strings, her face in rapture, I could imagine what she must have looked like in her previous life, young and beautiful, without a care in the world. It must have been wonderful to live life with the thought that one had the luxury of playing music without worrying about how to find money or food.

Some of the kids, including Abu, provided the percussion, using upside down *baldi*, metal pails or empty kerosene tins as their drums. It was not just community time, it was also family time, parents and siblings sitting outdoors in the soft evening light to do something enjoyable together. Karim sang with a sonorous voice and he made tears fall with his rendition of another of P. Ramlee's song from the film, *Ibu Mertua-ku*, *My Mother-in-Law*.

Everyone applauded when he finished. His singing was followed by two neighbours who recited a *pantun*, a folk poem, which took the form of a question-and-response style. Everyone was amused by their repartee. Then someone sang a *keronchong*, a plaintive Malay folk song, singing of heartbreak, loss and pain. Perankans also love the *keronchong* and would sing it at events. It was a wonderful evening of sharing and laughter. Music seemed to have the capacity to unite people, forging togetherness in a way that surmounted race, colour, creed or social status.

"*There is no magic like music for making an effect upon the human soul*," said the Sufi Master, Hazrat Inayat Khan.

"Shall we end the evening with something funny?" Karim asked. "I'm going to sing something written by my idol, Encik Zubir Said. He's from Minangkabau and is the music composer for Cathay-Keris Films. The two songs he did for the film *Sumpah Pontianak*, or *Curse of the Pontianak*, were sung by the *satay*-man. These acted as comic relief from the horror."

So Karim sang the song about *satay*, what it tasted like, how to make it, how to eat it. Silly but jolly stuff that made everyone laugh. He could have been an actor. When he said the word, *pontianak*, I became scared. She was the legendary female vampire. People who lived in kampongs heard about her all the time. Perhaps the stories were told so that parents could ensure that children did not wander around the village at nights in case she appeared! Yet the Pontianak was a recurring subject for local films. It seemed perverse that people were afraid to encounter a *pontianak* in real life, but loved the horror of seeing her on celluloid.

"You should give up your filthy job and play music at *Happy World*," Pak Osman said to Karin.

"Yes, yes," everyone agreed in unison.

"It's my life-long dream," Karim sighed. "But it's so hard to get the chance to get into a band."

Nearby *Happy World*, set up in 1936, was located between Mountbatten and Geylang Roads. It was the nearest of the *'three worlds'* to our village. The other *worlds* were *New World* on Kitchener Road and *Great World* on River Valley Road. These were places which offered affordable entertainment to ordinary families with children. In each world, there was a cabaret for adults, who could buy tickets to dance *ronggeng* with girls, circus and game-arcades for children, shopping for the ladies, and food stalls. Sometimes when my father received his annual bonus from the English firm he worked in, he would take us to *Happy World* or *New World* for a treat.

"Well you're certainly not going to be recognised for your talent shovelling shit all day. You must go there and make contacts. Show people how good your playing is. You might be lucky and run into the Soliano brothers or Alex Abisheganaden or someone else just as famous. They could take you under their wing and be your mentor," Pak Osman said. "Think positive. Dance-halls need musicians. If someone falls sick, you could be there to take over."

"That's a good idea," Karim said, his eyes brightening.

"Why don't we all go and support Karim?" my eldest brother said. "We can all have a fun night out."

Eldest Brother was addressed by us, his siblings, as Eldest Brother and not by name. In Teochew, he was addressed as *Ah Hiah*. That was our custom. He was twenty-one, and was thirteen years older than me. Eldest Brother was dark brown like me. He had just started work as a teacher at St. Andrew's School across the Kallang River from our kampong. Just as it was entertaining to watch my mother dressing to go out, it was amusing to watch my brother, as he spruced himself up for his trip to the cabaret. He slicked the thick *Brylcreem* pomade onto his hair and twisted his forelock into a Tony Curtis quiff. Tony Curtis, the handsome American actor, had a smile that would melt most women's hearts – and some men's too. My brother tried to emulate the smile in the mirror, making me burst into hysterics.

"Why? You think I'm not as handsome as Tony Curtis or what?"

He put on his Chinese New Year clothes, a newly starched shirt and his drain-pipe trousers. With his good looks, he was sure to catch any girl's eye. Then he doused himself with 4711 *Cologne*. He obviously bought it at the *Thieves Market, Robinson's Petang*, in Sungei Road – the real thing would be beyond his wages.

4711 Original Eau de Cologne was one of Cologne's oldest internationally famous brands. Called *Das Wunderwasser* or *Wonder Water* in German, its unique fragrance was said to refresh the mind, body and soul. The cologne was packaged in a distinctive bottle with a blue and gold label. Eldest Brother perfumed the air and me with its light fragrance. Feeling generous, he took the bottle of cologne with him and stepped outside.

"Hey, Karim! Come! I'll let you have some of my cologne so you won't smell of shit!" Eldest Brother called out.

The other young lads were all dressed like him and wore their hair like him. "So long as he does not end up like a *pondan* or *mafadek!*" One of them said.

Pondan was Malay for an effeminate man and *mafadek* meant *gay*.

"Oh, don't be like that," Karim responded good humouredly in a falsetto voice, gesturing with his hand affectedly. It made everyone laugh.

"Now don't touch any alcohol!" Pak Osman warned as the young men departed. Here Pak Osman was using a colloquial expression − *to touch alcohol* means to drink it.

Of course, by the time they got home, I was fast asleep.

So it became routine for Karim to try his luck at *Happy World*, hoping that his talent would be noticed. He spoke to members of different bands and stayed back late to help them pack their instruments. This meant that he was getting less sleep, as he had to wake up early to do his rounds of swapping the buckets of waste matter. He whistled less and less as he worked. He was transforming into a disgruntled person. It was also rumoured that he had taken to drinking *toddy*, the local palm brew, as well as hard liquor at the club.

But the transformation of the country was a positive one, fuelled by the previous year's announcement that Singapore was now a city state. Excitement rose to fever pitch when it was announced that there was to be an election in May. Posters of candidates were nailed to posts and walls. Electoral lorries with huge banners and people shouting slogans from megaphones trundled down the dusty, pot-holed roads of villages like *Kampong Potong Pasir*. A platform stage, similar to the ones put up for *China Wayang*, the Chinese Operas, held in the lunar calendar's seventh month to appease the *Hungry Ghosts*, was erected for the political rallies. The different parties presented their case. The most memorable speech was by the young lawyer, Lee Kuan Yew, from the People's Action Party (PAP). Nearly everyone in the village turned up in the vicinity of the badminton court, which served as our community centre.

My father carried me on his shoulders and was accompanied by his friend, Ah Gu, as people jostled for a view of the young man on the stage. He was dressed in a newly starched white cotton shirt and trousers. He was tall and slim, and possessed a very distinctive forehead. We had heard that he was educated at Cambridge University in England so we expected him to act very *atas*, or high-brow, and speak to us in the Queen's English. Instead he spoke to us in Malay and Hokkien, the lingua franca of ordinary kampong folk, making us warm to him instantly.

He had an arresting charisma and demeanour that made us feel that he was one of us. He shook hands with farmers, labourers and ordinary kampong-folk – and even with the likes of Karim, who handled buckets smeared with faeces. No one was too low for Lee Kuan Yew to shake hands with.

"If you vote us in, we will improve your lives," he said. "We will focus on making you comfortable; give you electricity and water in your homes; better schools, better job opportunities, better hygiene and better nutrition."

Similar words had been uttered by other politicians before and so were not radical or new. But this young man injected warmth and sincerity into his voice, making his promises, as if personally, to each one of us. His eye contact with everyone was steady, suggesting confidence, but it did not feel aggressive. His energy on stage was electrifying. No one could see him that day and not be affected. People were ready for change and we saw in him that instrument of change. The kampong folks hooted their approval, and when he raised his fist and cried out *Merdeka!*, everyone shot a thicket of fists into the air, shouting the word for independence over and over. We in turn were infused with tremendous energy and a sense of elation.

We heard that Lee Kuan Yew did not relax in his arduous campaign. He went round the whole mainland and outlying islands in this same charismatic manner, visiting kampongs and charming the ordinary folk, making people believe that our dreams for a better life were possible. He was our saviour for he promised liberation from our poverty, from our disgusting outhouses, from our lack of everyday comforts. He held high hopes for us. Hope was a jewel for the spirit. Without hope, people living in difficult circumstances would give up. He showed us an avenue of escape. So it came as no surprise that on May 31, 1959, his party, the PAP, won 43 out of 51 seats, to form a new government.

"The people's verdict is clear and decisive," the new Prime Minister, Lee Kuan Yew said. "Nothing more can be added to it."

He was only thirty-six-years-old and already held the weight of our country's development on his shoulders. Cries of *merdeka* exploded around the country, together with fire-crackers which strewed the streets, walk-ways and open grounds with their red splintered paper. According to Chinese folk-lore, the sound of exploding fire-crackers would scare the devils away; perhaps in this case, we hoped it would scare away the *Red Devils, Angmoh Kwee*, our rulers for so many years. The carpets of red were an auspicious symbol of prosperity and good luck. This was a country on the brink of nationhood. It was not yet completely independent but it was slowly yet surely making its way there.

In June, people were given the opportunity to apply for Singapore citizenship. For those who were born in the country, it was automatic but those who had resided for more than two years were also eligible. Six stamps were issued to commemorate this momentous event. Although the stamp still bore the Queen's head, it was designed with a Lion's Head as well.

"Isn't this marvellous?" Ah Gu said, showing off the stamp to everyone in the village. He had queued for hours to get it. "Our Lion City."

"Yes, we should be proud. We can finally call ourselves citizens of Singapore," my father said.

Even Karim lost his defeatist outlook. He had become dejected at not being employed as a musician but now the aura of hope in the country helped to blossom the hope he once held in his heart. In this new milieu, everything was possible. Education was possible for the masses, talent could be rewarded.

"It's good that you've given up drink," Pak Osman said. "You might think that alcohol helps you to be creative but in actuality, it's destroying its very essence. Don't squander your talent!"

"Thank you for your confidence in me, Pak Osman," Karim said. "Your belief in me is a treasure. I'll try not to disappoint you."

"Believe in your music," my mother told him. "Let your joy flow into it and you will bring joy to others. That is how success comes, not through your grasping but through your sharing."

Once again Karim whistled whilst he worked.

One day, he returned from the sewage works at *Kolam Ayer* with great joy.

"My idol, Encik Zubir Said's song has been selected as our new national anthem!" He announced. "It was a song that was composed for the Victoria Hall Chamber Ensemble for its re-opening. It's called *Majulah Singapura*, or Onward Singapore!"

"Do you know the tune and lyrics," the kids asked Karim. "Can you teach us?"

"Yes, it was on *Radio Singapore*."

The radio station had only been renamed that January, claiming its independence from *Radio Malaya*.

So the children, including myself, gathered round him as he strummed his guitar and sang out the Malay words, *"Mari kita rakyat Singapura* ... Come, people of Singapore..."

People of Singapore. It was a new, intoxicating concept. Somehow, under the colonial rulers, Singapore did not seem to belong to us. Now it felt different. The words of the song aroused in us a patriotism we had never felt before. It was *our song*, for *our own country*. For the first time, we saw the possibility that Singapore could be truly ruled by our own people. Indeed the lyrics fostered a feeling of togetherness, important for a country divided by different races clinging to their different cultural origins.

"Interesting that they did not choose a song in English," Ah Gu said.

My father's friend had a propensity to appear whenever there was political talk. He spent evenings with my father discussing politics.

"*Aiiyah*, Ah Gu!" My father said with some exasperation. "With all your lust for independence, I would have thought you'd understand straightaway. Using English, we would still be yoked to colonial power. Malay is the indigenous and national language of the region, so it is right that we should express our national dream in a local language."

"Of course, of course!" Ah Gu slapped his forehead. "I suppose the new National Anthem will replace *God Save the Queen*...?"

"Sometimes I am astounded by your stupidity," Ah Tetia said haughtily.

In July, Karim came home with news that his dream to play in a band had been realised.

"I shall play the guitar in a real band," he enthused. "There is going to be a huge celebration to commemorate the inauguration of our new government. It will take the form of an event called *Aneka Ragam Rakyat*, or *People's Cultural Event*, in August, to be held at the Botanic Gardens. There will be music all day so they need extra musicians."

"What did I tell you?" My mother said, her happiness for another's good fortune lighting up her face and making her look exceptionally beautiful. "When you infuse joy into your music, others can hear it and feel the joy too."

"My prayers for you have been answered," Pak Osman said with a smile. "I have made offerings to *Allah*, for you. I don't know how many chickens I have slaughtered for you! Hopefully, your exposure at this event will lead you to a more permanent contract. Then you don't have to shovel shit anymore."

There were many *firsts* in 1959. It was the first time the words *Radio Singapore* were spoken. It was the first time Prince Philip visited Singapore. It was the first time the PAP formed a government. English, Malay, Chinese and Tamil were made the four official languages and used in the Legislative Assembly. It was also the first time a local-born *Yang Di Pertuan Negara*, Yusof bin Ishak was installed, displacing the last British Governor of Singapore, Sir William Goode. Encik Ishak, a former journalist, was descended from a Minangkabau nobleman and was born in Perak. He began his education in a Malay school in Taiping and subsequently in Singapore, and was a student at Victoria Bridge School and the Raffles Institution. His intelligence and integrity made him the appropriate choice as the new head of state.

Most important of all, 1959 was the year when the Singapore flag was first unfurled. A committee headed by Dr Toh Chin Chye, Deputy Prime Minister and one of the founding fathers of Singapore, designed the flag. Its red colour represented universal brotherhood and equality for all men; its white part was a symbol of purity. Against the vibrant red of the upper sector of the flag lay a crescent which signified a young, fledgeling nation. Cradled within this crescent were five stars which represented democracy, peace, progress, justice and equality. People viewed the flag with awe and pride – it was our first and all our own. It was not just a piece of insignificant fabric; it was an enormously powerful symbol, invested with our hopes and dreams for independence. The new flag was hoisted up the flag pole at City Hall amidst much boisterous cheering – and down came the British Union Jack that had flown over Singapore for one hundred and forty years.

It was a great moment, the beginning of a new era and the first sprouting of our country's new identity.

A view of Great World Amusement Park, 1950.
(From the National Archives)

A Sense Of Identity
(1960)

IN OUR KAMPONG, we lived and worked together as one large, friendly community, but at the same time we celebrated our ethnic diversity. Malay, Chinese, Peranakans, Indians and Eurasians lived next door to each other without rancour, our doors open to each other. The common language that united us was Malay, so that everyone could communicate with each other. Several English families lived at *Atas Bukit, or* 'Top-Of-Hill', the hill above our village, in their 'black and white' houses. But they were not part of our community; they neither ventured into the kampong nor were they seen outdoors often. Occasionally when they had their garden parties, my friends, Parvathi, Fatima, and I, attracted by the English music and songs and the prospect of good food, would scramble up the hill to get a closer look.

Atas Bukit was our treasure-trove for fruits and food. There were mango, *rambutan* and *chikku* trees in the English people's gardens. When in season, the pendulous branches, laden with fruit, would hang over the garden fence, where they were easy to pick. When the acid in your stomach grinds your insides due to lack of food, high morals fly out of the window.

The English looked incongruous in our environment, deathly pale in our strong sunlight, as if they had just emerged from spending years in dark underground caves. In Malay we call them *Orang Putih*, White People, but in Hokkien and Teochew, we call them, *Angmoh*, Red-Haired. We can only guess why. But unkind and disparaging people used the term *Angmoh Kwee*, meaning Red-Haired Devils. Their women wore large-brimmed hats and pretty dresses, their men wore cream linen jackets. We skulked round corners and hid behind lamp posts and trees as we did not want to be discovered.

"They think we're vagabonds and thieves," our parents drummed into our heads. "So don't disgrace yourself by being seen!"

"Hello! Welcome! Glad you could make it," a man said in his rich voice.

"*Darling*! How wonderful to see you," a lady replied.

I loved the English accent, the way the words rolled on the tongues of the English people. The rhythm of their language was delightful. Not like the way we spoke English here. *RP* it was called. *Received Pronunciation.* Or BBC English. Their men had such deep voices. I spied one who could be my next heart-throb, once my crush over P. Ramlee was over. He was very tall, had blondish hair, with forelocks which swept down over his forehead.

But my priority at that moment was food. Our eyes feasted on the long table resplendent with all kinds of nice things to eat, large turkeys, meat joints, sausages and pies. There were also European fruits like apples, pears and oranges – the kind of fruits you would find on the shelves in *Cold Storage*, a special supermarket on Orchard Road, catering to the *angmohs*. One of the ladies in our village, Fauziah, who worked there as a shelf-stacker, said that there was cool air-conditioning in the supermarket. She also said that there was a room kept at freezing temperatures to house their winter coats made of fur and animal skin, which they needed when they visited England. It was a concept beyond one's ken. I surveyed the table for

Cold Storage specialty items – rashers of bacon, meat pies and tempting delectable cakes of many varieties.

"Oh isn't it nice to be so rich?" Fatima said.

"Look at that! Men and women mixing and chatting together as if they were equals!" Parvathi said with incredulity.

There was an obvious inequality amongst the village folks between men and women, and particularly for Parvathi's people, who were Indian. Gender roles were more marked in our day.

The day after the English parties was a feast day for us.

When I was only five, Third Elder Brother taught me how to scour their rubbish bins safely to find our treasures. Now that I was nine, I was already an expert, making sure not to plunge my arm into the bins but to slowly pick up each item layer by layer, in case there was broken glass or dangerous things like knives hidden amongst the rubbish. The day after the parties lots of uneaten food was thrown out. Of course some food items were unsalvageable, but food like cakes could survive if left in tins or wrapped well in baking paper. Fruits and vegetables like apples and carrots, luxury items for us, were also hardy enough to survive being chucked into bins. Hunger meant that you could not afford to be proud. The positive aspect about being deprived is that everything you get is a bonus. So getting even ordinary or small things can make you joyously happy.

"Be careful of the Alsatian!" Third Brother warned me.

Now that I was older, he was confident enough to let me go on my own. One of the English families kept an Alsatian dog, which guarded the premises vigilantly, and it nearly bit off my arm once when I tried to steal its lunch – a huge steak.

My friends and I came back from this particular round of scavenging with a whole packet of boiled sweets, fairy cakes still in their waxed-paper cups and a train set with some carriages broken. But my prize was an Enid Blyton book, *Five Run Away Together* from her *Famous Five* series, complete with illustrations. It was slightly the worse for wear, but I did not care. I enjoyed the stories in Enid Blyton's books and dreamt about the kind of life she talked about and the privileges the children in her books had. It was my dream to go and live in England where I would always have food to eat. Now that I was in school, I could actually read the words in the books, whereas earlier I could only look at the pictures. I was overjoyed to be educated. It was the unexpected fulfilment of a dream.

"Will you read it to me?" Parvathi said, wistfully.

She was tall and beautiful, four years older than me. Despite her family's poverty, her hair was silky and luxuriant, and her eyes, ringed with kohl, were large and black. Parvathi had never been to school. Since she started menstruating, her father, who was nearly always drunk, kept on threatening to marry her off to an older man. As she was the eldest child in the family, she had to go out to work so that she could help bring in money to buy food for the family and medicine for her younger brother, who suffered from fits. Many village children had to work to help their families. I sold the nonya *kuih* and *nasi lemak* my mother made, to get money for me to go to school. Other children helped out at food-stalls, collecting bowls and plates after customers had finished with them; some washed other people's clothes, worked in shops, sweeping floors, some at the rattan factory, weaving baskets or mats. Parvathi worked at the paper factory in the village, folding squares of paper into envelopes. The process had not been mechanised yet. The crisp new paper was so sharp that it often cut her hands in many places.

"I wish we could run away together," she said when I read her the story. "Then we can have an adventure and I won't be forced to marry."

Many uneducated girls in the kampong were still subjected to arranged marriages. As soon as they became teenagers, their fates were sealed. That was why I was so grateful that my mother had fought for me to attend school. Otherwise my fate would have been like theirs – although my father still threatened to marry me off as soon as I was eligible. But like Parvathi, I had planned to run away if my father forced me to marry. Except that I did not want to hurt my precious mother.

"What are ham rolls?" Fatima asked when she heard that Julian, Dick and Anne, the English children in the story, ate ham rolls and drank ginger beer. She was a Muslim and proclaimed that she would never drink an alcoholic drink like *ginger beer* and weren't Western children liberal to be drinking beer at their age? She, like Parvathi did not go to school.

Of course I hadn't a clue either but I did not want to look stupid.

"Some kind of meat," I said. "Hmm, chicken is from hens, beef from cows, so ham must be from hamsters."

"What is a hamster?" Fatima wanted to know.

"A kind of animal-*lah*!" I said exasperated, not wanting to show my lack of knowledge. "The kind of animal that lives in

England, obviously! Don't ask stupid questions-*lah*! Wouldn't it be good if we were boys rather than girls. Women don't seem to have fun in life. Look at our mothers, they work day and night, feed the families, wash clothes, have babies. I want to be a tomboy like George. Then I won't have to always listen to and obey my father and brothers. I want to think for myself. Have all kinds of adventures. Maybe I should be called *Jo* instead of *Phine* so that I'll sound more like a boy."

"The trouble with you," Parvathi said with a wisdom beyond her years, "Is that you don't know who you want to be. Girl or boy. Chinese or Malay."

"*Ya-lah you*!" Fatima said. "No wonder the kids in your school call you OCBC."

There was a bank in Singapore called the Overseas Chinese Banking Corporation, or OCBC in short. So some cruel kids in school played on the initials of the bank to make fun of Peranakans.

They jeered, "*Orang Cina Bukan Cina*." The words translated as *Chinese person, not Chinese*.

My friends were right, I was undergoing an identity crisis. I wanted to belong. When you belong you are part of a whole. When you don't belong, you are an outsider. Whether other Peranakans felt this dichotomy of identity or not, I was not sure. Perhaps it was just my own personal angst. I had a Chinese surname, celebrated the Chinese New Year but I did not look Chinese or speak Chinese. Our family did speak some Hokkien and Teochew, but not Mandarin. Sadly, though deep brown, I did not look quite Malay either. I would like to have had their more pronounced facial features, larger eyes with proper eyelids, better noses and high cheekbones. I felt like I was in no man's land.

"Okay-*lah*," I said decisively. "I want to be a boy. And I want to be Malay. From now on, call me Osman! Or maybe a Malay girl, Salimah."

"You see what I mean?" Parvathi said. "You don't know what you want!"

The girls giggled till their sides hurt. When the laughter stopped, Parvathi went quiet, her face thoughtful. A cloud of sadness swept over her face. Then she lashed out in a harsh voice.

"*Aiiyah!* Crazy idea! Do you really think women can choose to be what they want to be? Look at the women in this village. Do you think they choose to be here, in these circumstances? Choice for women is a fantasy!"

"Come on," I said. "We can still pretend! Or hope."

"Let us go and watch the men prepare their birds for the *Perkutut of South East Asia Competition*," Fatima said, trying to defuse the situation.

A *perkutut* is the generic name for *burong merbok*, an Asian kind of dove. *Burong* is Malay for a bird. There was an annual competition to find the bird which sang the sweetest. Training birds to sing was our kampong men's favourite pastime. Likewise in other kampongs. It was a pastoral activity. The majority of the men were Malay. Malays had a marvellous yen for creativity and were very much in touch with their softer side. They were known to maintain beautiful homes despite their material lack. To them, it was not a waste of time to admire birds and train them to sing.

My mother constantly told me, *"You are never too poor to not be clean or not be creative."*

"Yes, let's," said Parvathi. "The beautiful singing will cheer me up."

We found the men underneath the huge canopy of the banyan tree which gave them shade from the hot sun. The tropical fig tree had aerial roots that were so firm they looked as if they were propping up the tree. Long strands of thick vines grew down from the branches, the type that I imagined the body-builder Johnny Weissmuller swung from in his role as *Tarzan* in the films. The tree's leaves were large and elliptical, silky and deep green. Many of these trees loved being by the water so the moist banks of our Kallang River were most suitable for their growth.

My friends and I gasped in amazement at the forest of hanging wooden bird-cages, hoisted on tall poles, with a bird or two in each of them. The men, who were mostly bare-chested or in singlets and sarongs or drawstring shorts, were sitting, watching or coaxing their bird to sing by whistling. The scene was idyllic, a sense of peace prevailed, the birdsong generating an aura of tranquillity. The birds sang in different keys, creating a sweet symphony of sound. It was a rural delight.

One of the men was Pak Awang. People say that when Pak Awang's mother was giving birth to him at home, he slipped from her hold in a slippery trail of blood and body fluids right onto the cement floor, knocking his head before the midwife could rescue him. The incident caused Pak Awang to act in a different way from other people. He was in his fifties then, yet had the innocence of a young child. Luckily he was well looked after by his siblings and one of his younger brothers, Hassim, was there with him. It was lovely to watch Pak Awang whistling and coaxing his birds to sing.

"*Burong nyanyi! Burong nyanyi!* Bird singing! Bird singing!" Pak Awang repeated with simplicity, complete concentration on his face.

"Abang Hassim," Fatima addressed Pak Awang's brother with the polite Malay honorific *abang, Elder Brother.* "Where will the competition be held? And when?"

"The bird singing contest will be held in May at Buona Vista." Hassim said. "There'll be hundreds of entries from all over Malaya, Indonesia and Sarawak. Three winners will win the silver cups. The birds will be judged on the clarity, sweetness and strength of voice. That's what Awang is doing, training his birds to exercise their vocal chords. He may not be good at anything else but in this he seems to do well."

Buona Vista was in the West of our island, a short distance away from Pasir Panjang with its golden sandy beaches and attap houses on wooden stilts. Nearby, the British army had its barracks. Buona Vista was chosen for the competition for its setting of beautiful woodland, majestic rain-forest trees and flame-of-the forest trees, with their spectacular crown of brilliant red flowers.

"His eyes are shining!" I said.

"Yes, this is what makes him most happy. It gives him a sense of identity," Hassim said. "That's why I bought him the birds so that he has a purpose to his life."

"You're a special brother," Parvathi said.

"No, not me," Hassim shook his head and pointed to Awang. "He's the one who is special."

"*I need someone like him to rescue me from my fate,*" Parvathi clutched my arm and whispered to me.

In our adolescence, we had talked about our dream to be rescued by some knight-in-shining armour, a concept I picked up from reading the books discarded by the English families. But it was a faraway dream. Parvathi's tragedy awaited her. She had no opportunity to marry for love. I too felt her sorrow. Women seemed helpless in the face of destiny. Parvathi was doomed. All her father cared about was easing his own burden by marrying her off as soon as he was able to.

My father often said to me, "I shall marry you off at seventeen! Then you can be a burden to your husband, no need to waste more rice and money on you."

My father, and Parvathi's father, often used words that cut into our psyche. They said things which made us feel unwanted and unloved. To our fathers, we were chattel, to be traded or sold. But Ah Tetia's moods swung like a pendulum. Sometimes he could be so nice, cooking breakfast for the family or bringing home a packet of *Hokkien-Mee* noodles. The *upeh*, the bark from the Betel-Nut Palm helped to keep the noodles warm and moist all the way home, and its woody fragrance flavoured the noodles in a special way. Usually his mood was buoyant when he got his wages from the firm he worked for, or when he was carrying weights in the sandy yard with Rajah and Salleh. That morning, they were discussing Singapore's hopes in weight-lifting at the Olympic Games.

"Tan Howe Liang is going to the Olympics to try for a medal," My father informed Rajah and Salleh, who could not read the newspaper.

Tan Howe Liang was Singapore's weight-lifter. He had won a gold medal at the British Games in 1958. This year the Olympic Games were to be held in Rome.

"Maybe got a chance," Salleh said.

"Aiiyoh! Very hard-lah!" Rajah said. "He has to compete with Westerners! Like the Johnny Weissmuller type. How can he win?"

Pessimism hung like a pall over our country as well. Our new country was wrestling with its sense of identity. We were toddlers in nation building, not yet steady on our feet, self-governing but not yet totally free. The elation of the previous year when the PAP came to power was darkened now by problems. There was a shortage of food, housing and jobs. The story that dominated the *Straits Times* newspaper was that of Mr Tan Kok Thuan, who was forced to give away his six children aged five to sixteen because he could not afford to feed them.

In the newspaper report, it was reported that he said, "All I ask is that they should be given a good education and that my wife and I be allowed to visit them."

It was a story that touched many hearts. A Malay woman came forward and offered to marry off the two elder daughters, one to her son and the other to a cousin.

Our family felt his pain keenly. We too had been in such dire straits that a child had to be given away. I thought about my own brother with sadness, the one whom I did not know, the one who was given away at a time when my father did not have a job. People born to riches will never experience such separation nor know this kind of sorrow. Luckily for Mr Tan, lots of donations came in after the newspaper article so he did not have to give his children away.

The first of June was to be our first national day. A big parade was planned for an all-day celebration. But it rained – and rained. The heavy raindrops dug potholes in our sandy village road and turned clay into a slippery sludge. Though challenging to walk on with flip-flops and shoes, it provided us village children with an opportunity to compete in a made-up game, sliding on the wet mud in our bare feet to see how far we could go without coming to an abrupt halt.

"Look at me!" Abu, Fatima's brother yelled merrily as he slid down the muddy pathway or *lorong*, his legs and bare torso completely splashed with mud.

More rain cascaded into our houses through the broken attap roofs. Shouts to get buckets and pails were heard all along our row of terraced houses. Rain drummed loudly into empty pails and kerosene tins, followed by the 'glug-glug' sound of water as they filled up. Our *longkang*, drains, which usually helped with the drainage, could not cope with the heavy rain and started to fill up, and turned into gurgling brooks.

"I have an idea," said Parvathi. "Let us make paper *sampan* boats.

A *sampan* is a traditional Malay wooden sailing craft which fishermen used for going out to sea. Parvathi went away and came back with an armload of old newspapers and scrap paper which she got from the factory where she worked. Deftly, she cut and folded paper as if creating an origami and presented us with her finished result – a little paper boat complete with a sail! We were impressed. So we followed her instructions and other village children joined us.

"I know," said Abu who had an entrepreneurial streak. "Let's have a race. Winner gets a boiled sweet."

So we launched our paper sampan boats and cheered, running alongside the drains as our boats coursed through the swirling water in the *longkangs*. Like all poorly made craft, some of our boats tumbled and sank – their owners crying out in despair. But some actually survived the white-water roiling of the drains and made it all the way into the big pond.

But the flood waters continued to rise dangerously in our Kallang River, flooding the vegetable farms at *Lai Par*, the inner sanctum of our kampong. Luckily it did not reach our houses, but it brought the smell of rotting vegetables and the stench of manure and faeces. It also destroyed the crops, which meant more hardship for the farmers. Other rivers in the country, like the Bedok, Hougang and Punggol Rivers were also affected, swelling to disproportionate levels. In Punggol, there was an added problem, as the murky waters brought back the Punggol Crocodile. It was reputed to be twenty-five feet long and weighed six hundred pounds, and caused as much fear as the python which had plagued our kampong earlier. The dense vegetation surrounding the banks of the Punggol River gave the reptile places to conceal itself. People panicked. Professional hunters were sent out to capture it. They went armed with shot-guns and busy-bodies from our village went to watch the hunt.

"There it is!" someone shouted.

True enough, the crocodile's long snout rose above the dull-coloured water exposing its head and beady eyes. Confident that it was safe, the crocodile crawled up onto the river bank on its stubby legs to sun itself. The hunters aimed and fired. But the crocodile's rough skin was so thick, it acted like armour and the bullets ricocheted off its back, merely tickling it! It was never caught.

The water also rose in the Bukit Timah canal, the huge canal which divided Bukit Timah and Dunearn Road. My father could not go to work as it would be too dangerous for him to cycle in the flood. The rising waters flowed over the canal and hid it from view, so people and cars fell into the canal. *The Straits Times* had a front page photo of a car floating down the swollen canal like a rudderless boat.

So the national day parade was cancelled.

"It's a bad omen for the country, "Ah Gu said.

Ah Tetia's friend was one of those who seemed to thrive on dramatising misfortune, like a black fly feeding on a cow-pat.

"You think that's bad," my father said with some annoyance, proffering the newspaper. "Look at this. The island of Ceylon is appointing Mrs Sirimavo Bandaranaike as prime minister. She will be the world's first female head of state. What the hell does a woman know about governing a country? She should just stay at home and look after the children!"

My father's chauvinistic attitude was not uncommon amongst men of his time. But despite male opposition and disapproval, the tide had invariably turned. All over the world, women were coming into the forefront of society. In Singapore, the breaking news was the appointment of a local female director, Mrs Hedwig Anuar, to be in charge of the new Raffles National Library which was built in red brick on Stamford Road. A graduate of the University of Malaya and also educated in London, she was a petite, attractive and intelligent woman who was unafraid to speak out. She gave local women a new sense of identity. We admired her.

Mrs Anuar was instrumental for much of the change in reading habits. She wanted to make reading accessible to everyone, particularly those who could not afford to buy books. She took books and the library to the poor with her mobile libraries. When the first cream-coloured van with the words *Mobile Children's Library* written on its side panel trundled down our village, we hailed it like it was some kind of messiah. The driver of the mobile library had to negotiate the potholes in our sandy kampong road. We watched with interest and worry as the van waddled from side to side in its journey to its berth. Thankfully the driver was skilful and he managed to get it parked on the concrete badminton court next to our community centre, which had the only bit of hard surface where it could stand on solid ground. The library assistant threw open the back doors and it was as if a new universe was being opened to us. Lined on either side of the inside of the van were shelves and shelves of books.

"Wah!!" Everyone exclaimed, impressed by the van's contents.

For people consumed by the idea of basic survival, a book was an item of luxury which they could ill-afford. For the majority of us, to own a book for leisure purposes was an impossible dream. So we queued dutifully to take our turn to walk up the steps into the library. My entry into it was as magical as stepping into a fantasy kingdom. When my mother had taken me to Bras Basah Road to buy my school-books, I had fallen in love with the touch and smell of books in the bookshops – and now I fell in love all over again, but with a greater impact, like a thousand volts shooting through me as I stood there inside the van, surrounded by precious books! The scent was intoxicating. The library was an Aladdin's Cave of treasures, unexplored worlds, places and people crammed into the pages. I wondered what the Raffles Library on Stamford Road must be like with its thousands of books. I hoped to visit it one day. I felt overwhelmed that it was our new government that was providing all these books for free. During the political campaign the previous year, PAP had promised that they would make our lives better. And they had kept their promise. We could escape from the dreariness of our lives through myths, fables and fairy tales. I took out another *Enid Blyton* book for myself and a large picture book for my mother.

"Ah Phine," she said. "Tell me where this place is. Read to me. I didn't send you to school for nothing."

And so began my life-long habit of reading to her – books, magazines and newspapers. She had a voracious appetite. And so too began my life-long fascination and love-affair with English words, the way they were used and their subtleness of expression. I was amazed at how a squiggle of printed words on a page could influence the way I thought or felt.

"Okay," Pak Osman said. "Make sure that you are all ready to help build the road. The Municipal is delivering the sand and gravel as promised and we have to spread it over our potholes. Don't wear your best clothes when you turn up!"

The new government was fulfilling yet another of its rally promises. They were true to their words about helping to improve our lives. Our village people were touched that they had not forgotten their promise. Most politicians make all sorts of promises during their campaigns, but once elected, they seem to forget or choose to forget what they had promised. But the PAP didn't. They were going to help us repair *Jalan Potong Pasir*. The word, *Jalan* could refer to the Malay verb *walk* or the noun *road* – more specifically, a *village road*; its usage in context determined its meaning. A city road which is tarmacked is often known as *jalan raya*. Huge potholes meant that it was difficult to navigate our road; taxis charged more to come into our village. So we were overjoyed. Truckloads of sand and gravel arrived at our kampong. As usual Pak Osman took charge of harnessing the labour force, as he did in 1957 when our village was plagued by the tyrant *Ular Sawa* python.

It was heartening to see the spirit of the villagers, men, women and children who turned out to help. Malay, Chinese, Peranakans, Indians and Eurasians. People came with spades, *changkols* and whatever could be used to dig and even out the road with the sand and gravel provided. My parents, brothers and I went along too. Even Pak Awang came, accompanied by his ever-vigilant brother, to help in the road-building.

"*Saya pun mahu tolong*," Pak Awang insisted. "I too want to help."

So his brother Hassim let him scoop the sand. The sand was brought out of the trucks by the *samsui* women who carried the sand in wicker baskets on their heads. This special breed of women, mostly spinsters from mainland China, was robust and uncomplaining. The women wore their characteristic dark blue *samfoos* and red square hats. Then we dug and filled the numerous potholes with gravel and poured sand all over the village road. We stamped our feet to flatten the fill. The dust flew, making us cough, and our clothes were coated with fine sand-dust, making them grubby, but we were happy as it meant that we would not have any more potholes for a while and the mobile library could navigate its way more safely. Old men and women brought drinks for those who laboured. Hawkers plied their trade alongside, supplying us with snacks and food as we worked. One of my favourites was steamed chick peas, called *kachang kuda* in Malay, in chilli sauce, sold by the *kachang puteh* man. I had no idea why the *kachang* or nut was called a *horse nut* though I understood that the hawker was called after a type of nut he sold, which was white with a glaze of sugar. People sang and laughed as they worked. It was hard physical work but it was also like a festival. The task gave us a sense of identity as a community. This was *gotong royong* at its best, people working together for a common goal.

"Look what I've found in the library," Parvathi said excitedly. "These fashion pages are lovely!"

Parvathi was holding the first ever copy of *Her World*, an Asian woman's half-face large on its front page. It was the first national magazine devoted to Asian women, beauty, health, crafts and domestic issues – an innovative idea for our times. Parvathi turned the pages whilst we oohed and ahhed. There were centrespread photos of beautiful models in gorgeous clothes. It was as if the magazine was showing us an ideal world where women could have what they wanted.

"*Alamak!* It costs seventy-five cents *lah*! Who will buy it?" Fatima said.

"But there are lots of pages with articles and stories and lovely photographs."

Yet I understood Fatima's sentiment. When a packet of *nasi lemak* or a bowl of noodles cost ten cents, spending seventy-five cents on a magazine seemed frivolous.

"A magazine just for women? The world is truly changing," my mother said.

"Parvathi!" I said as the thought occurred to me. "This shows that women are getting more freedom. We don't have to be shackled to old ideas anymore. If there can be a woman who runs the national library and another a whole country, there is hope for you."

"It's too late for me," Parvathi said, melancholia dragging down her cheeks. "Until they bring in a law preventing men from having as many wives as they like, or a law preventing parents from forcing their daughters into marriage, or one which makes parents send their children to school, how can there be hope for people like me? I'm doomed."

"You are only thirteen! How can you be doomed?" I said, almost angry that she would give in so easily. "You have to fight injustice! You have to fight your father!"

"*Aiiyah*, Phine," she said, smiling slightly. "You're still so young..."

"But you are young too! You are only thirteen..."

"...I like your enthusiasm. You have fire in your belly. Mine has gone out. What choices do I have without any education? Your mother is so right to persevere and send you to school. Education is your hope to get out of your circumstances and this village."

Sadness and lack of opportunity made Parvathi old before her time. Deep inside me, I knew she was right. I could weep for my friend. I was so lucky to have a mother with such foresight. Parvathi's mother was exactly in the same position as her daughter, uneducated and without choices, not the kind of living that any daughter would want to inherit. Like many men, her husband had other wives and other children. There was no law to protect women like her.

Rajah and Salleh, who carried weights with my father in our sandy backyard, knocked on the wooden posts of our kitchen excitedly. The young men were tall. With their dark brown bodies, they looked like heroes who had strayed from a Shaw Brothers film-set. During the *gotong royong* event when we were building our kampong road, I had seen how their bare bodies had glistened with sweat as they dug and filled the potholes in our road.

"*Encik* Chia! *Encik* Chia!" they called out to my father. "Have you heard the news-*lah*? It was on *Rediffusion*! Tan Howe Liang has achieved his dream! He has just won a silver medal at the Olympics!"

"Wow!" My father beamed. "He has made us proud. It is our country's first Olympic medal. The competition is very tough. For us to compete against big-size Westerners is already a huge step forward. To come in second is truly amazing! He will definitely go down in history!"

But Pak Awang was not so lucky. His birds did not win any prize in the bird-singing competition. He came home with his head bowed, his lips pursed.

"*Tak menang*," He grumbled. "*Tak menang*. Did not win. Did not win."

Floods hit Kampong Potong Pasir, 1954.
(From the National Archives)

Pond-fishermen rearing fish at Kampong Potong Pasir, 1956.
This pond was later filled to make way for public housing
by the Housing Development Board.
(Courtesy of Lim Kheng Chye)

The Burning Question
(1961)

D.H. LAWRENCE'S INFAMOUS book, *Lady Chatterley's Lover,* was banned in England but managed to slip the net and found its way into Singapore. Published by Penguin, the novel was derided for its explicit depiction of the relationship between the lady of the manor and a gamekeeper. Perhaps it was the novel's audacity to suggest a transgression of the British class system that offended? The burning question was, was the book as racy as was suggested? Readers in Singapore wanted to find out. After all, forbidden fruits were said to taste better. Fuelled by the fact that it was a banned book, locals flocked to Bras Basah Road, bookshop haven, to buy the book, which cost only a dollar seventy-five. The bookshops sold five hundred copies in two weeks. People read the book with its covers clad in brown paper.

My father would kill me if he knew that at ten, I was reading romantic novels! To be more precise, Parvathi chose the novels and I read them to her. Half the time, I did not understand the subtle nuances. I simply read the English words. It was my first realisation – one might have the capacity to read but not the capacity to comprehend.

The books we read furtively were not even remotely close to *Lady Chatterley*! They were rather tame. Their covers often displayed a Western man and woman staring into each other's eyes. So I did what all my classmates did, which was to wrap the covers in brown paper. There were romances of doctors and nurses, highwaymen and ladies, and blockbusters by Barbara Cartland and Denise Robbins. Innocent stuff actually – no graphic description was given when there was a mention of a kiss. If anything more than the touch of hands was alluded to, the line would go ************. Or as we mimicked: *asterisk, asterisk, asterisk*. You had to read in-between the asterisks and use your imagination. Sometimes this was much more wild than what the author might have intended!

"If only there was someone who could take me away from my fate," Parvathi said in earnest. "Then I won't have to marry that pock-marked old man my father wants me to marry! Do you know that the man is twenty years older than me?"

My Indian friend was fourteen. She still could not read as she had never been to school. Going to school was a luxury and privilege many village children did not have. The romance books were her only escape from a life of work, drudgery and squalor.

"Your father is crazy! You can't marry an old man..."

"Some of us have no choice...," Parvathi sighed.

Karim, our village singer and musician started sporting a new hair-style. He used to work as a night-soil man, clearing the buckets from the out-houses, but he was now a fully-fledged musician. In 1959, he had performed at *Aneka Ragam Rakyat*, *People's Cultural Event*, which was a huge celebration held at the Botanic Gardens to commemorate the inauguration of our new government. There he was 'discovered', and was offered a full-time job as singer and guitar player in the *Great World* cabaret on River Valley Road. Now his dark hair was thick with *Brylcreem* and his forelock was swept down over his forehead.

"What happened to your Tony Curtis curl?" My Second Elder Brother asked.

"*Aiyyah*! That's out of date, now it's all Elvis Presley-*lah. Are you lonesome tonight? Do you miss me tonight*," he crooned à la Elvis.

The American singer was said to gyrate with his hips and was considered obscene by some. Compared to him, people found the British singer, Cliff Richards, more acceptable, as he looked more like the boy-next-door. However, Elvis' voice was creamy and seductive, so his songs were still a big hit on *Rediffusion*.

Eldest brother had used part of his teacher's salary to have the cable radio installed in our house. It was our village's first step into modernity.

Next to books, listening to the *Rediffusion* was the second great delight. It opened up other new worlds to us. We heard what was taking place around the country through the news, enjoyed listening to the disembodied voices coming into our home bringing in all sorts of information, all sort of music. Elvis, Cliff Richards, Frank Sinatra and local singers like my idol, P. Ramlee, Anneke Gronlo and Susan Lim entered our homes to entertain us. But not everyone in the kampong could afford a *Rediffusion*, so many of the kampong neighbours came to sit in our house when the news came on. Our house became like a community centre. Then for the first time, we heard the voice of Tunku Abdul Rahman, Prime Minster of Malaya, who urged Singapore to merge with Malaya to become one big nation.

"*...We have to make Malaya our one and only home.*"

"He means that he does not want Singapore to identify with the Chinese communists," Ah Gu, who was also listening, elaborated profoundly. "He is cautioning us. With more Chinese than Malays amongst us, he's afraid we might become a *Little China*."

Ah Gu, if you recall, was my father's friend, who popped by on a daily basis to discuss politics with him.

"The idea makes sense," Krishnan our Indian next door neighbour, said. He rarely joined in the kampong activities, but the *Rediffusion* had attracted him, and like my father, he was one of the rare educated men in the village. "Singapore was part of the Straits Settlements and part of Malaya as far back as we can remember. Yet the British gave them independence in 1957 and not us, so suddenly we were left out. Merger with Malaya would make us part of the same whole again."

"True, true," Pak Osman said. "I felt like a limb was cut off when we separated from the Federated Malay States..."

"We're so close geographically, it does not make any sense for us to be separate nations..." My father said.

Our own Prime Minster came on air, "...*the solution to Singapore's future lay in a Common Market and merger with the Federation...*"

We liked Mr Lee Kuan Yew as he had personally visited our village during the elections, and we felt as if he was our own hero. We were convinced that he truly wanted to improve our lives – and he had done so, first the filling up of pot-holes in our village road, and then the Mobile Library, which brought us books.

The topic of the merger was hotly discussed amongst the menfolk.

My mother and the other womenfolk provided them with snacks like *apok-apok*, our Peranakan *kueh dada* and the *bandung* drink made out of Rose Syrup and evaporated Carnation milk whilst they themselves clustered in the kitchen, sitting on the hard concrete floor, to talk about the price of food, the difficulty of bringing up water from the well during the drought, and naughty children.

The burning question was – do we or do we not merge with the Federation of Malaya, Sabah and Sarawak to become an integrated nation? But this issue was not the only hot topic of discussion. The weather was too. It had been a very, very hot March, stretching into a sultry April. The white sun bore down relentlessly. Clothes hung on lines dried quickly, the home-starched bed-sheets became stiff like paper, and the attap on the roofs became dry and crusty. We had only one well which served the entire village, and this too was fast drying up. The catfish kept at the bottom to eat up the mosquitoes became so thirsty and lacking in oxygen that they died and floated belly-up on the muddy bit of water that was left. The stand-pipe was at least a quarter of a mile away and its water was regulated so that it was used only for drinking water. But the reservoirs were drying up too, so the water that ran came out of the pipe was slowly reduced to a brown trickle.

We prayed for rain.

Normally the frogs in the ponds would croak and croak and the villagers believed that they were calling for rain. But now, even the frogs were sullen and silent. Even Nenek Boyan, who was supposed to have descended from the tribal *batak* people and was reputed to practise witchcraft could not persuade them to croak. So she suggested a different solution.

"Thread some whole chillies and onions through a stick and place them outside your front doors and it will bring rain." She advised.

So, speared into the sandy threshold outside every front door of the village was a kebab of fresh chillies and onions. Still the rain did not come. The village *bomoh*, the medicine man, danced and waved his arms at the clouds and chanted. But the rain still did not come.

The previous year, we were plagued by floods and now in contrast, we were suffering from drought, our rural lives governed by the capriciousness of the tropical weather. The *padi* or rice fields, which were usually flooded for the first seeding, were dry, their mud bunds cracking with dryness. The kampong's four ponds shrank, leaving an edge of exposed bed where some fish could be seen floundering and flipping themselves in a frenzy of thirst. People became listless from the heat, leaves and flowers sagged with exhaustion. More people slept outdoors, on roped *charpoys*, folded canvas camp-beds and woven straw mats.

I wondered how the English people at *Atas Bukit* were coping with the heat. The scorching sun must scorch their fair skin and blind their pale blue eyes. Their delicate constitution was not made for our harsh heat.

The attap-roof, woven from palm leaves, exposed day-in, day-out to the blistering sun, became drier and more brittle. All it took was the weight of a small starling walking across it, and the attap would cave in and break, creating more holes in the roof. The attap was quickly becoming a safety hazard, poised for becoming potential kindling. A broken piece of glass caught in the folds of the attap could attract a ray of sunlight and burst into flames. The attap-roof and the wooden walls which our houses were made of were easy to burn. As kampong houses were sandwiched tightly side by side, a single spark could spread like wild fire in dry grass.

One night one of our neighbours, two doors away from our house, was smoking when he fell asleep. The lighted cigarette butt fell onto his pillow and started a fire. His attap-roof rapidly went up in flames. My parents woke us sleepy children and ushered us out of the house hastily. The small passageways or lorongs between the houses made it doubly dangerous as they became packed with people trying to run away from the fire. Luckily the fire was contained very quickly. When the drought persisted, villagers ground their cigarette butts and matches into the sand; and practised extra care to extinguish coals in stoves, candles and oil or kerosene lamps. In heat waves, the normal precaution was to douse the attap roofs with water, but we were rapidly running out of water. What made it worse was that we were running out of fresh water to drink. Our throats were parched.

The government had to intervene.

"The water truck is here! The water truck is here!" A child shouted with glee.

Like a gargantuan messiah, the Municipal Water Truck trundled down our sandy village road. It was greeted with greater joy and relief than the Mobile Library. It was a monster of a truck in size, huge with hundreds of gallons of water, the flexible hose behind it like the trunk of an elephant. We placed our pails and empty kerosene tin-buckets in line to be filled. The driver rationed the water. Each household was permitted only two buckets of water. Second Brother carried our share of the precious water home carefully and proceeded to store it in our giant, Aladdin-type of earthen jar called a *tempayan*. Each night before we turned in to go to bed, my mother would place empty pails and buckets outside the house in case it rained so that we had water for our washing and cleaning.

"*Mari kita mandi dalam kolam*! Come let us bathe in the pond!" Abu suggested.

Abu was the elder brother of my close friend, Fatima, and he seemed to have a commanding air about him. If he had been educated, he would probably be successful.

Normally our parents would not permit us to bathe in the ponds. Firstly because the muddy pond-bed was dangerous as it could suck us in. And secondly, it was not exactly hygienic, since the people who lived on the edge of the ponds had their latrines positioned over the pond and they would defecate directly into the pond. One of the village children's past-time was to go and watch when someone was doing a *big job* just so that we could see the fish appearing suddenly. As someone pooped and the waste matter plopped into the water, shoals of fish rushed up from nowhere to stir the murky water to feed on it.

"No thanks," I said. "I will wait for rain."

Still the rain did not come. By May, we were so hot that we slept with our doors open wide to channel in any little breeze. Of course that let some stray dogs into the house, like the one who was slobbering all over me whilst I was dreaming of P.

Ramlee. The worst thing was the rats which came in from the smelly drains and fields.

"The government is negotiating with Malaya to buy more water from Johor," the newsreader announced on *Rediffusion*.

As a small island with no fresh water rivers to speak of and only four main reservoirs to supply the country, we were in the unenviable position of having to buy our fresh water from Malaya. Malaya was our hinterland and the Peninsula, with its spectacular mountain ranges and natural fresh rivers and waterfalls, stretched all the way north to Thailand. When we were part of the Federated States, it did not pose any issue to share the water as we were all the same nation. But now that we were not of the same nation, it became more of a concern. So perhaps merger with Malaya would be wise.

On Thursday, May 25, President John F. Kennedy of the United States announced in front of Congress his plan to put a man on the moon. It was a hugely ambitious dream. We could not even fathom such an idea. What would they use to go to the moon? A very special aeroplane? Having a *Rediffusion set* in our house meant we learnt about things we would never have known about otherwise. Modern technology had brought the rest of the world closer to us.

On the same day, in our village, where the residents were mainly Malay, we were celebrating *Hari Raya Haji*. This was not a huge affair like *Hari Raya Puasa* which commemorated the end of the fasting month of Ramadan, but instead this was mainly confined to those who had completed the *Haj*, a religious pilgrimage to Mecca. People like Pak Osman who had done the pilgrimage wore a *songkok* or white cap on their head, to denote that they were *hajis*. On this special day, they had to make a trip to the mosque. After that, they would celebrate by sharing food with neighbours. In our kampong, each of the different races made a point of sharing food with the other neighbours on their new year. I absolutely loved the custom as it meant there was food to eat.

Pak Osman's wife made the most delicious *ketupat*, rice cakes made from boiling rice in coconut-leaf bags for hours. These were cut into cubes and eaten with her superbly mouth-watering mutton curry and *selondeng* or fresh grated coconut fried in aromatic spices. The juices in my mouth ran whilst waiting for the food to be delivered into our home.

It was in the afternoon, whilst we were in this joyous mood, that we heard the terrible news that came over *Rediffusion*. An attap-kampong, similar to ours, located on the Bukit Ho Swee hillside in the central part of our island, had caught fire. The village was not far from River Valley, where Karim was rehearsing for his performance that evening. We knew from our own kampong that their village would be tightly packed like ours, so a fire in this scorching heat would mean that their attap-roofs were very dry, so they would act like kindle, and the fire would spread very quickly. The other reason for its spread is that, like our kampong, there was probably no running piped water in the houses at Bukit Ho Swee. Like us, they had to rely on wells and a standpipe that was some distance away. So it would be a huge task to put out the fire easily. We could easily imagine how terrified the villagers must be.

We curtailed our celebrations and huddled around the *Rediffusion* to wait for more news. We became more worried when the reporter said that a strong wind was picking up in that part of the island, fanning the flames as they crackled across roof-tops and wooden walls. Before long, we did not even have to sit by the *Rediffusion* to understand the extent of the fire, because outside, huge clouds of black smoke were billowing into the air. We could smell burning rubber. The fire had spread to a rubber factory where sheets of latex waited to be processed. The stench of burning latex was horrid.

Throughout the day, the fire burned and spread. There was a stark band of bright sunlight above the tree-tops, but beyond that the sky was dark as the winds took the smoke up higher.

Karim came home to tell us how he witnessed the raging conflagration.

"It's horrible! Horrible! There were minor explosions. I think when the fire got to the oil mills and motorcar workshops. When it ate up the timber-yard, the flames grew brighter and became huge, red and orange. The fire engines were screaming their way to the kampong, followed by the police and ambulance. It was chaos. I don't know how the people are going to run away..."

We had experienced a kampong fire before, and though ours was small, we knew what it would be like, people trying to escape via the narrow lorongs in panic, bumping, squashing and falling over each other. We knew that the kampong at Bukit Ho Swee was much larger than ours and had well over two thousand attap-houses, jammed tightly together, each wooden wall and attap-roof feeding the fire's voracious appetite. Our hearts were filled with sorrow. We could only listen to the *Rediffusion* and watch the sky darkening deeply, and pray that the people, especially the children, had time to run.

Next day the female announcer's voice was sombre, almost trembling as she reported the aftermath, *"Four people died in the Bukit Ho Swee fire yesterday and eighty-five have been injured. Sixteen thousand people have been made homeless..."*

Considering the circumstances, it was astonishing that more people had not died. Thank goodness. But sixteen thousand homeless! It was a tragedy on a huge scale! It was our country's worst kampong fire. It decimated the whole village and relegated it to the annals of history.

The government had the huge task of finding housing for all the homeless people. It was one of the PAP's biggest challenges. Although the smoke eventually disappeared and the smell in the country returned to normal, there was a dark pall hanging over the nation. But other compelling issues surfaced for the PAP. The bid for merger had caused dissension. Certain people expressed dissatisfaction with the government, making allegations of victimisation and unfairness. The previous year, the Minster of National Development Mr Ong Eng Guan had formed a break-away political party, the *United People's Party*. Then Dr Lee Siew Choh formed the *Barisan Socialis (Socialist Front) Party*.

But it was not all doom and gloom.

1961 was the year when significant changes to the law made life more tolerable for women. The *Women's Charter* was brought in, making it illegal for girls under sixteen to have sex or to be married off. This spared Parvathi temporarily from being married to the pock-marked older man. Men were not permitted to marry many wives and were now financially responsible for their first wife and children. There was more protection for women and children against abuse, especially physical abuse. But though this was made legal, it was still not easy to implement, as women like Parvathi's mother or my own mother would not have the wherewithal to report such cases.

Though those of us living in the kampong would never dream of aspiring to go to University, we cheered when we heard the news that a woman, Professor Dr Winifred Danaraj was appointed Chair of Social Medicine at the University. She had graduated from King Edward VII College of Medicine, which was established in 1905 as the Straits and Federated Malay States Government Medical School. She was awarded a Fellowship in 1950 and was also a Queen's Fellow. She had also been a Postgraduate of Harvard School and London University of Public Health. First Mrs Hedwig Anuar, who became in charge of our National Library, and now, Dr Winifred Danaraj. They were our trail-blazers.

It gave us other women a chance to dream. We had not dared to hope before, especially those of us who were brought up in poverty and in the villages, under strict rules made by our fathers, uncles and brothers. Now it looked as if there was a small window opening, a window that was allowing light to pass through so that women did not have to remain subjugated by men. It was a significant moment for young women like us.

Maybe life could be different for young girls like Parvathi. All was not lost.

For the first time in our lives, we felt that we could really aspire to be what we wanted to be.

Kampong boys playing at a stand-pipe, 1950s.
(From the National Archives)

Changing Times
(1962)

THE NEW YEAR began well indeed. Our own university was born. What used to be a division of the University Of Malaya now became the autonomous, fully-fledged University of Singapore. Appropriately, the inauguration took place on January 1 at the Bukit Timah campus, just off the eponymous road. Built on a forested hill, the placement of the white buildings was reminiscent of classical British institutions of learning, with a clock tower, arched corridors and quadrangles opening onto manicured lawns.

Every time we had a *first*, whether it was the *first* university or the *first* local head of state, it reinforced our identity as a self-governing country, free from the clutches of colonial power. Like a toddler who has to discover his own confidence and ability to walk, our country too had to find its steady feet.

My father, who worked in Bukit Timah, had to cycle past the university campus each day, and he told us how awe-inspiring it looked. This was spoken by a man who did not think that women should be educated! Luckily, my eldest brother did not share our father's limited view of women.

"Come on," Eldest Brother said to me. "Let me teach you a game."

He taught mathematics at St. Andrew's School, which was just across the river from our village. Eldest Brother liked games that tapped his left brain and had an analytical edge. He produced a wooden board that had black and white squares on it. The board was placed on a disused orange-crate. The slatted crate once held oranges that were sold in the market. These empty crates became our tables or chairs, since we could not afford real furniture. Then Eldest Brother took out the beautifully shaped wooden figurines from the box and set them on the board. He had found the set at *Robinson's Petang*, the Thieves Market at Sungei Road, by Rochor River. Someone had playfully nicknamed the outdoor bazaar after the most expensive English department store on the island, Robinson's; but added a twist in *petang*, which meant *afternoon*, to suggest its lack of authenticity – and the name had stuck. Eldest Brother displayed the two sets of figurines, one opposing the other.

"This game is called chess," he said with authority.

He patiently told me the name of each piece, its position on the board, the direction it could move, and its role. I was amazed to learn that all the pieces on the board existed to protect the King. Once the King was unable to make a move without being taken, he was considered to be check-mated; and the game would end. It was such a novel and bizarre concept for me that I became riveted to it.

"I thought men are always the ones who protect the women? How come the King can only move one square at a time when the Queen can move any number of squares? Is the Queen more powerful than the King?"

"If you stop jabbering, I'll explain how the game is played," Eldest brother said, with some impatience. "This game was conceived in India and was styled after a battle. Maybe they had a matriarchal society then."

Though I was hopeless at maths, I loved the game – it was so exciting, with so many different moves and permutations. And secretly, I loved the fact that it was the Queen, the woman, who had the most liberal moves on the board.

"Not bad, not bad," Eldest Brother said when we played. "Maybe you'll be our *Girl Wonder*."

"What's that?" I asked.

"Oh, it's a play on words," said my schoolteacher brother. "There's a student whose name is Tan Lian Ann and he's been nicknamed *Boy Wonder*. He represents Singapore in the chess championship and he's only fourteen! He just beat defending champion R. E. Fontana in the Malayan Chess Open in KL."

"Wow," I said. "It shows we don't have to be limited either by age or by gender."

Teaching me chess was Eldest Brother's greatest gift to me. It became my life-long passion. Not that I played well enough to join in any competition, but it gave me hours of pleasure. Later I told my best friend Parvathi about the rudiments of chess.

"Imagine a woman being more powerful than a man!" I said.

"Huh! That's only a game," she snorted. "It's not like real life, is it? In our world, our fathers and brothers control us and tell us what to do, how to live. If the *Women's Charter* had not come in, my father would have married me off last year when I was only fourteen! To a pock-marked man who's twenty years older than me!"

We looked at each other. The image of that pock-marked old man with the bad teeth must have flashed across our mind's eye at the same time. We giggled. It was a shared moment of intimacy. Of course we could laugh because we thought the danger had passed for Parvathi.

But for someone who had no schooling, her prospects were indeed dismal. However, I kept on trying to reassure Parvathi that times were changing and that women were getting opportunities they never had before. When I read in the *Straits Times* about Ong Cheng See, our first local female graduate to be admitted as an advocate, I raced to tell Parvathi about it.

"You see! You see!" I said exuberantly. "We have another woman who has broken the traditional mould! If we can have women as lawyers and as prime ministers, it means you can break out of your mould and not be forced to marry."

"How?" She asked, her eyes flashing. "How? When I work in a paper factory? I've no spare money and no education. Those women had rich parents who sent them to school and university!"

Our village was not more than ten miles from the city, but in many respects we seemed worlds away. The difference between the rich and poor was a greater chasm than our huge monsoon drains. Now that I could read the newspaper, I realised that our kampongs were sometimes perceived by city folk as ghettoes, where street urchins ran riot, where filth and germs perpetrated, where gangsters hid, and where the *pontianak*, the female vampire, still roamed.

People fear what they do not know.

Krishnan, our Indian neighbour who worked with the 'Municipal', usually kept himself apart from the other villagers, as he was educated and was a Brahmin. But on this day, he dashed out to the sandy yard where my father was lifting weights with Rajah and Salleh. It was late afternoon, so the long shadows provided a cool shade. Even the chickens, ducks and dogs were enjoying the coolness.

"I have good news, I have good news," Krishnan announced.

At that moment, Ah Tetia was lifting some heavy bar-bells. He put them down cautiously with the help of Rajah before he sat up. He used a hand towel to wipe the sweat off his bare chest. The towel was thin, with some swallows and Chinese characters printed on it. It was an iconic piece of towelling, as it was used widely by coffee-shop owners and hawkers, who slung it over their shoulders.

"Mr Krishnan," Rajah addressed him respectfully just as he did with my father. "What's all the excitement about?"

"The government is going to provide us with a generator so we can have current!" He patiently explained the function of a generator and kept using the word 'current' for electricity. "We will have to fix wires and fluorescent tubes in our houses, so that when the generator is turned on we will have light! In the beginning, we will only have light from 7PM to 9PM. But it's a good start-yes?"

"Yes, yes!" Everyone agreed.

The news spread round the kampong quickly. People rejoiced.

But my father's friend Ah Gu practised restraint. "People don't give anything for nothing. I wonder what the PAP wants from us."

"Gu-ah!!" My father retorted vehemently. "For once – can you be positive? The PAP has done nothing but keep their promise to make our lives better. Don't you remember that last year they gave us all that material to repair our village road? They also sent the water-truck promptly during the drought..."

"I still think it has to do with all this talk about merger with Malaya. Lee Kuan Yew wants us to agree to his plans. You must be aware that the *Barisan Sosialis Party* is opposed to the idea...?"

"Gu-ah." My father said. "You know the *Barisan Sosialis* has communist tendencies. Just because you are Chinese-educated doesn't mean that you have to adopt their view. Don't you think the PM is right? Merger with Malaya, Brunei, Sabah and Sarawak will make us into a bigger, stronger nation. We're only a little island. Last year we had to buy more water from the Malayan Federation to survive. If we belonged to the same nation, we wouldn't have to worry so much when we needed water!"

"It's true," said Pak Osman, who appeared and joined in the conversation, nodding his head. "All of us used to be part of the Malayan Federation. It's more natural for us to be part of the same nation than apart. Come, come. We have work to do if we want to get the current into our houses."

Once again the villagers joined in with the *gotong royong* spirit, working together as one community. Wooden posts sprouted from our kampong soil like magic trees, their lines of electrical wires like the vines of the banyan tree. A naked bulb stood atop each of the four posts. The technician came to install the apparatus in our house. Thick, black cables snaked their way at the top of our wooden walls to the fluorescent tube. The long strip of bulb looked strange against the naked attap rafters. It seemed like an invasion of a foreign being who had come to stay.

The villagers congregated for the first lighting of the street lights.

"You see," Ah Tetia said. "The new government is fulfilling its promise to make life better for those of us in villages."

"*Huhh*," Ah Gu grunted.

He sounded more like a pig than the cow he was nicknamed after.

The generator roared into life. The electric bulbs pulsed. Then the light came on. For us who had existed for years on kerosene and hissing carbide lamps, it was a tremendous moment. Mak and I used to embroider and sew *manet* or plastic beads onto Peranakan slippers in the shifting flames of the oil lamps. Our eyes used to get so tired from the strain. Now we would be able to see our handiwork more clearly. So it was not a moment that we would forget easily.

"*Wahh!!*" Everyone exclaimed as the first electric light came on to dispel the darkness. But it was short-lived.

The generator grumbled and then went off. We were plunged into inky blackness. People groaned. Someone lit a candle. Then the generator was restarted with belching rumbles, and the light came back on. That was a pattern we became used to. We were lucky if we got a whole hour of electricity per evening. Most of the time our candles, hurricanes, carbides and oil lamps were on standby. But still we were grateful – something was better than nothing. Finally our kampong had a taste of modernity.

On August 2, there was an announcement on the radio; "*Britain has agreed in principle to the formation of Malaysia and would hand over the sovereignty of Singapore, Sarawak, Brunei and North Borneo to the Malaysian Government on August 31, 1963.*"

September 1 was proclaimed as the day when the citizens of Singapore were to vote on the terms of the merger, in the *Singapore National Referendum* or *Merger Referendum of Singapore*. Many of the uneducated villagers were perplexed, so they came to my father to ask for clarification. Everyone sat outdoors in the sandy yard including Karim, our resident musician and singer, and Pak Osman, our village leader.

"Basically, you have to put a tick on one of the three options. One is Option A. Here you choose that all Singapore citizens would automatically become citizens of the new nation, Malaysia. But Singapore will still retain some say in matters such as labour policies and education. And we'll also keep our four major languages, English, Mandarin, Malay and Tamil as our official languages. Because in Malaya, Malay is the official National Language. Two is Option B. Singapore will become a federal state of Malaysia. So Singapore will be no different from the other eleven states. That means we will have to give up control over issues such as labour and education policies to the federal government in Kuala Lumpur. Also, no multilingualism – only English and Malay will be used for official purposes and in schools. Three is Option C. Singapore will enter on the same terms as the Borneo territories, Brunei, Sabah and Sarawak."

When my father finished explaining, the group talked amongst themselves, discussing the various options.

"Option A makes sense-*lah*! We can be part of a big nation but we will have our own say and won't lose our identity," said Krishnan. "Tamil will still remain an official language."

"*Ya-lah*," Everyone agreed.

"How come there is no option *not* to join the merger?" Ah Gu had to put the spanner in the works. "Maybe, just turn in a blank vote or what?"

"It's a vote, so it's your choice. But think carefully before you put your *dhoby-mark*. It's for the future of the country," my father cautioned him.

My father was using an analogy for the tick that would go on the voting form. He was referring to the spot of black dye that launderers or *dhoby* workers put on the underside of clothes to identify their laundry, when they used communal drying areas like at *Dhoby Ghaut* near Selegie Road, where the washing was strung out on lines that stretched across the small wood of trees. In time, the term *dhoby-mark* also came to mean the signature impression that one made, as in, "he put his dhoby-mark on the way the factory was run".

In November, the Commonwealth Games were held in Perth, Australia. Formerly known as the British Empire Games, the new name was a reflection of the changing times. My father read the news to his weight-lifting mates, Rajah and Salleh, with great joy.

"Tan Howe Liang has won a gold in the middle-weight division. He lifted 860 pounds! And Chua Phung Kim grabbed a gold in the bantam-weight division."

"*Wah*! Two gold medals in one championship!" Rajah exclaimed. "Times are changing for us."

In December, a different kind of gold was won. The elation over the acceptance of merger with Malaysia by the majority of the people put the authorities in a congenial mood. So when the new dance craze, *The Twist*, hit Singapore cabarets and clubs, they did not ban it, although there were murmurs that they might. Chubby Checker of USA, whose real name was Ernest Evans, sang the song, accompanied by a twisting of his pelvis, more seductive than Elvis'. The dance demanded great flexibility, as one had to twist right to the floor and rise up again whilst twisting. It was certainly very energetic and it made people perspire profusely in our heat and humidity. Some people deemed the movement too risqué and seductive. Eventually, the government made an announcement over the radio: "*So long as it remains a dance and is not sexually or morally depraved, we will not ban the records or films.*"

"Hurray!" Everyone cheered.

Karim, who worked at the Great World Cabaret, came home and taught us the dance. He strummed his guitar and sang the hit song, "*Let's do the twist…*"

The villagers turned out to watch. Children and youngsters like Parvathi, Fatima and myself rushed to the sandy yard to emulate him. Our elders stood outside the ring, watching us.

"*Macham orang gila!* Like mad people," they said with half-smiles.

But we did not care. We shook our heads and hips and thrashed our arms about to the rhythm of the music. Our frenzied dancing frightened the chickens and ducks. Even the dogs whined and crept under shelter. Our stomping feet in the sand raised clouds of dust that flew onto everybody's clothes. But no one minded, because in some ways, we were acting out the euphoric mood of the nation.

Second younger sister on a tree-trunk at a seaside kampong house, 1959.

Those Who Dared
To Dream
(1963)

MALAYA'S PRIME MINISTER Tunku Abdul Rahman and our own Lee Kuan Yew had a shared vision of a united Malaya and Singapore. Before Malaya became independent in 1957, the Federated States of Malaya and Singapore were considered Malayan. These two visionaries saw that it would be advantageous to be one again. They were men who dared to dream. But sadly, there were many others who tried to thwart their dreams.

It should have been a year of joyous anticipation and rejoicing.

After all, since 1959, when we attained self-government, we had looked forward to the time when we would have full independence. This was finally going to happen on August 31, 1963. Britain had agreed to hand over the sovereignty of Singapore and North Borneo to the new Malaysian government. But there were blots on the political landscape. The *Barisan Sosialis Party* of Singapore had already made apparent its disapproval of the merger. Now our neighbouring countries of Indonesia and Philippines also spoke out against it. The Philippines had revived an old claim to British North Borneo, whilst President Sukarno of Indonesia desired Malaya and Borneo as part of his own territory. As early as January, after one of his aides returned from a meeting in Beijing with Chairman Mao, President Sukarno said that the formation of Malaysia was not acceptable and he would react with *konfrontasi*, the Indonesian word for *confrontation*. He sent troops to North Borneo and even into Malaya. Disturbances erupted here and there.

British troops had to step in to provide assistance.

Those who dared to dream pushed on – their dreams were a bright beacon of light in the darkness that enveloped us.

I too harboured a dream. It was a preposterous dream.

I dreamt of being a writer – in English.

Ever since I had encountered the English language, I was filled with a kind of joy that was indescribable. I loved its cadence, its music, its depth and subtlety of meaning. I loved the Janet and John books, Enid Blyton's famous books, and every storybook I could get hold of. I even enjoyed the romantic novels that Parvathi made me read to her. I loved the pleasure of forming English words to create stories. I was fluent and literate in Malay and could write essays and compositions, but it did not spark me to want to write books, as the English language did. So I started by writing a comic.

Parvathi brought me scraps of paper from the factory she worked in. I cut them into three-inch rectangles. I wrote a story in simple English for the village children and illustrated it myself with pencil drawings. I stapled the pages together and sold each for five cents. These were my first earnings as a writer!! Actually the five cents included my reading it out as well – if the child could not read!

"Hey, Phine! Your stories are good," the kids said. "Maybe you should be a real writer."

But I did not dare to share my dream with anyone. It would sound ridiculous. I was going on twelve. How could I know what I wanted to be? But I did know. Perhaps I had a prescience about my future.

1963 was a special year for me in the Chinese lunar calendar because on January 25 of the Gregorian calendar, the Lunar New Year that began would be a Rabbit Year. I was born in a Rabbit Year in 1951. Each new Chinese year coincides with the advent of spring in China so it is also called the Spring Festival. The night of the first day of the New Year has the new moon, though invisible, and the celebrations end on the night of the full moon, on the fifteenth day. The lunar calendar years are named after the twelve animals of the Chinese Zodiac. Folklore said that The Creator called the animals to him, and he named each year in the order they arrived: Rat, Ox, Tiger, Rabbit, Dragon, Snake, Horse, Sheep, Monkey, Rooster, Dog and Pig. This meant that one's animal birth year would only come round every twelfth year. If you reached the age of sixty, you would be in your Golden Year, which would be your fifth twelve-year cycle.

Each animal sign has its own characteristics, which are governed by its element which, in turn, has its own propensities. The Chinese birth signs relate to five elements: earth, metal, water, wood and fire. This meant that when you reached your Golden Year, you would enter the same element which you were born under. The year 1963 had the element of water. Mine was metal. Experts in the Chinese art of geomancy, *feng shui*, made their predictions based on one's animal sign, element, hour of birth and the *Kua* or *Auspicious Direction*.

We Peranakans celebrated Chinese New Year. Our culture was a mix of the Chinese and Malay. Most Peranakans started off as Buddhists or Taoists. I loved Chinese New Year, as it meant we got delicious food to eat, as well as new clothes. Peranakans, like many Chinese, were very *pantang* or superstitious. So they bent over backwards to fulfil every Chinese New Year obligation. Preparations for the New Year started weeks before the event. There were *kuih-kuih* or Nonya cakes to be made, new clothes to be sewn, furnishings to be changed, the house to be white-washed with *kapor* or lime-stone, and the cement floor to be scrubbed. It was a labour-intensive period, and everything had to be done manually.

My mother peddled furiously on her Singer sewing machine to make new clothes for my siblings and myself. As usual, she managed to find a bolt of fabric from *Robinson's Petang*, or the Thieves' Market. From experience, my brothers and sisters knew we would end up with matching dresses and shirts! My brothers were none too pleased when the fabric was floral. In bad years, when she could not buy enough fabric to sew curtains for the house as well as our clothes, she would hang up new curtains but use the previous year's curtains to make into clothes – so the clothes could still be regarded as new. It was imperative for each person to wear a new article of clothing on the first day of the Chinese New Year, to bring in good luck. Of course, black was a taboo colour as it was used for mourning. Although Mak made Western-style clothes for us, she herself wore only the *sarong-kebaya*.

"You father has given me some money to make a new kebaya for New Year," my mother told me happily. "Come on. You can come with me to Joo Chiat to choose the material."

Joo Chiat was in the Eastern sector of our island and was considered a part of the seaside village of Katong, the rich

Peranakan enclave. Many Eurasians also lived in the vicinity because of its close proximity to the sea and its luxury houses. The road and area of Joo Chiat was named after Chew Joo Chiat, a nineteenth Century Chinese trader who had married a Peranakan girl. With great foresight, he had bought huge tracts of land to grow gambier and coconut trees, which were highly valuable. These made him into a multi-millionaire. To cope with any possible threat of war, the British wanted to build a road that would run from the city to Changi, where they planned to build their sea defences. The road that ran through Chew's plantations was a dirt road. As military vehicles needed to travel on firm roads, the British offered to pave his road and to make it their main access road. Chew generously permitted this, and in recognition of his donation, the British named the road after him.

Our trolley buses had now been replaced by wireless buses run by the Singapore Traction Company (STC) and a local businessman, Tay Koh Yat. As red was an auspicious colour in the Chinese ethos, the *Tay Koh Yat* buses were all red. Without the massive network of overhead cables that had been used for the trolley buses, our skies looked a lot tidier. But there was an increase in the number of posts for street lights and electrical wires, which were creeping out from the city towards rural areas. Those of us living in the kampongs watched this slow advance with excitement, because it would mean the end of having to use our temperamental generator, and we would have consistent electricity. When electricity finally arrived in our village, we really celebrated. The PAP had certainly fulfilled its rally promises, which made us so joyful. We felt eternally indebted.

My mother and I had to change buses to get to Katong. Once we got there, I immediately felt the change in the air and could smell the salt. I gulped the fresh air repeatedly like a fish out of water.

"What are you doing?" Mak asked.

I answered, "*Makan angin.*"

To *makan* is to *eat*. And *angin* means *wind*. It was a metaphor for going for a stroll outdoors or having leisure time. But I was purposely interpreting it literally in an attempt at humour.

Mak laughed. It was so lovely when she laughed. Her life was so hard that she did not have many such occasions.

"*Di Tanjong Katong, airnya biru /*At Tanjong Katong, where the water is blue..." she sang softly.

The song was one of our traditional songs, and she brought the words to life with her melodious voice. Like Karim, our village musician, my mother had an innate sense of rhythm and style. I felt happy and sang along with her as I skipped down the palm-tree lined coastal path. The wind blew my hair about and I tasted the salt in the air. I fell in love with the sea yet again. Perhaps it had something to do with the fact that my solar astrological sign was Pisces. I loved the way the sea whispered as its waves rolled in and out. I imagined they were trying to tell me of places they had been to around the world, so I listened hard. The sea gave me a yen for travel, another of my dreams.

Most of the houses by the sea were made of concrete and were magnificent. They were big bungalows on concrete plinths, with stone stairs that led down towards the sandy beach. Like the terraced houses in Joo Chiat, the houses had ornate decorative designs and were in colours that were typically Peranakan – pinks, turquoise-blues and greens, so much so that some of the houses looked like iced celebration cakes. They made the whole area seem cheery and friendly. The terraced shop-houses were on two floors and sold all sorts of Peranakan food, ingredients and wares. Mak was in her element. Her face brightened tremendously.

"We must buy some *stangee*," she said. "And some *bunga rampai*."

Stangee is incense that is made from an aromatic wood, and *bunga rampai* refers to a potpourri of the petals of various flowers and shredded pandan leaves, mixed with essential oils. Both are the Peranakans' ways of keeping their homes smelling sweet and fragrant. Mak was in a celebratory mood and definitely feeling rich. Otherwise such luxuries were usually considered an extravagance.

At the corner of a row of shophouses, my mother treated me to traditional *nonya laksa,* noodles cooked in thick spicy coconut milk. We ate it with a spoon as it was the kampong way, though some people were beginning to adopt the Chinese way of using chopsticks.

At Joo Chiat, she trawled me through fabric shops and stalls in the market. She fingered numerous bolts of voile material. She was a skilful seamstress and could sew her own kebaya, though she would bring the completed kebaya back here to a specialist to *ketok lobang*. The latter was a row of fine holes, *lobang* in Malay, that were punctured into the fabric and they ran from the shoulder to the hem of the kebaya. They had no practical function but looked pretty. Either my mother or I would *jait sulam*, that is, embroider flowers and birds along the edges of the kebaya. It was a time-consuming process, so homemade kebayas tended to have just a simple row of embroidery. The more elaborate the embroidery was, the more valued the kebaya was deemed to be, as if it was a proof of the wealth of the people, who could afford to pay others to do it.

Finally she found a turquoise-blue fabric. She knew my father liked the colour on her. She found a *batik* sarong which had a pattern and colour which matched. We went home laden with our purchases, which included *gula Melaka* and flour for making the *kuih baulu, kuih tart* and *kuih belanda, serai, lengkuas* and *daun limau perut,* for the various sambals and curries. She was making all the various delicacies not just for our family but to distribute to the neighbours as well. My mother always put others first. But it was also a kampong tradition – the households celebrating their New Year would share their largess with close neighbours. This meant that we all joined in the celebration of the different races' New Years, which created a very convivial atmosphere in our neighbourhood.

On this Chinese New Year, Mak surprised me by giving me a small pair of hooped gold earrings, which was such an extravagance. She must have got her *senoman* or *tontine* money, the scheme of saving money along with a group of people that villagers bought into.

"This is your Rabbit Year, so it's a special gift." She said. "By the time your next Rabbit Year comes, who knows where I will be."

One of the delights of the Chinese New Year celebrations was the firing of red fire-crackers. If you laid your ears to the

ground as I did when I slept on a mattress on the floor, the distant
sound of the fire-crackers exploding was like the stampede of
buffaloes. The Chinese fired crackers to scare the devils away
from their homes. Because the fire-crackers were red and the
colour was auspicious, when they splintered, they sent showers
of red paper into the air, bringing good fortune into our lives.
These were never swept away during the days of celebration.
Besides, sweeping the floor on the first days of the New Year was
considered bad luck, as it meant sweeping away good fortune
from the home. The other delight was playing with *bunga-api*
or flower-fire. These were thin wires of fireworks that were not
explosive- they merely sizzled, and when we waved them around
in the dark they created delightful trails of bright light.

On February 15, there was another cause for celebration in the
country.

Television made its debut appearance. The thought of being
able to view films in one's home was a revolutionary idea. There
was excitement in the air. A broadcasting station was set up and
it was called *TV Singapura*.

My father took my mother, my two younger sisters and me
to the inaugural telecast outside Victoria Memorial Hall. We
went in a lorry together with other villagers from our kampong,
which included Ah Gu, Krishnan and his family, Pak Osman,
Karim, Abu, Fatima and their parents, and also Rajah and
Salleh, my father's weight-lifting mates. I managed to get a space
for Parvathi, though her mother did not come. Wooden planks
were placed across the back of the lorry and we used these as

seats. As there was no back support, if the driver went too fast, we would sway dangerously, so we had to hold onto the planks tightly. But we had a jolly ride, Karim entertaining us with his guitar and songs, which we joined in when we knew the words.

"*Long distance looking*. That's what *tele-vision* means," Krishnan showed off his knowledge.

Of course, important people were invited to be inside Victoria Memorial Hall. We were told that there were seventeen television sets in the hall. We were standing outside, where a marquee had been erected to protect the sets that were placed outdoors for us. There were hundreds of people. Everyone jostled and craned their necks to look. It was not easy for me to see anything. My father carried one of my younger sisters on his shoulders and Ah Gu carried the other.

"What about me? What about me?" I cried.

Parvathi was taller than me so she had no difficulty in peering over heads and shoulders. I really did not want to miss out on the historic moment. Karim took pity on me and hauled me up onto his shoulders, and when my elder brothers turned up later, they swapped over.

The TV was switched on and a clock appeared in black-and-white.

Everyone applauded and shouted, "Hurray!"

The hands of the clock ticked towards six o'clock. Our eyes were riveted on the clock as if it was a hypnotist's instrument. Then the clock faded and the Singapore flag appeared, but without colour, to the accompaniment of *Majulah Singapura*, the song composed by Encik Zubir Said, which was performed in public for the first time in that very hall. Everyone stood to attention and sang.

It was an emotional moment. Come August, we would be singing a different national anthem.

Culture Minister S. Rajaratnam appeared on screen and said in English, "Tonight might well mark the start of a social and cultural revolution in our lives."

He was followed by a documentary programme, *TV looks at Singapura*. This was followed by a cartoon feature, then a newsreel and a comedy. We were so engrossed, we did not realise the passing of time. Before the telecast ended, four announcers spoke in the four official languages to give a summary of the next day's programme. The whole thing lasted for an hour and forty minutes.

Of course, most people could not afford to buy a television. Certainly not many in our village could spend money that was meant to buy food. The Culture Ministry knew that the average citizen was not flush with wealth, so it proposed that bars, coffee-shops and restaurants should install TV sets for their customers. Transmission began with only one hour per day, but slowly the hours increased to four. People congregated at public eateries in the evening, where there was a TV set. The kids in our village acted as spies, and kept on the look-out to see which coffee shop or neighbour had bought a TV set, so that we could steal a view.

On my birthday in March, my father, who had never given me any presents before, surprised me by giving me one. It was a ten-cent stamp with a picture of a blue kingfisher, one of my favourite birds, on it. The thought went through my mind that it was a strange present.

"This is our new stamp which has just been issued," he said proudly. "Look! There is no queen's head on it anymore. From this month, all our stamps will feature local orchids, birds and fishes."

The light bulb went on in my head. Ahhh! Another historic moment. It was not just about stamps. The change might seem insignificant but it was actually a huge step that marked the onward progress of our nation.

Television impacted our lives in a way we had never dreamed possible. Just as libraries, books and *Rediffusion* opened up new worlds to us, TV *took* us there on a daily basis. Up until then, the only newsreels we saw were at the cinema in *Pathe News*, which were screened before the cartoon and main feature. So if we did not go to see a film, the only reports we received were from the radio and newspapers. Now far-off places were brought into our living rooms – at least for those who could afford a television set.

When Prime Minster Lee Kuan Yew came home from London in July after successful constitutional negotiations regarding Singapore's status within Malaysia, we could actually *see* the smiles and share in his triumph. It was due to this new medium that we could see Dr Martin Luther King deliver his speech to 250,000 people in Washington, USA, on August 28, starting with the words that became iconic, "*I have a dream...*".

"*Merdeka! Merdeka!*"

The shouts echoed across the country when Malaysia finally became a reality. What we had hoped and dreamed of for years was finally realised. We felt an emotional charge for our country, and a sense of identity was forged. Sadly, our neighbour Brunei had opted out of the union. So our new nation was formed of Malaya, Sarawak, Sabah and ourselves. This great occasion was marked with a new flag.

There was rejoicing but there was also an increase in tension.

This was the beginning of an infection that spread. For some reason, some Malays began to believe that Singapore joining Malaysia was only for the improvement of the ethnic Chinese community, so the worm of tension grew between the two races. Luckily for us, in our kampong we separated political ideology from personal relationships. But in kampongs like *Geylang Serai*, people who had once looked upon the other as a brotherly neighbour now looked at people of different facial features and colour with suspicion. Having lived peacefully with each other for years, people now became aware of others as different. The rot had started.

On September 7 we saw a telecast that unsettled us. In Jakarta, Indonesia, Anti-Malaysia rioters burned down the British Embassy. And on September 24 two bombs went off in Singapore, then another in October, all in the Katong area. An innocent girl was killed near Jalan Eunos in another blast. People were thrown into a state of unease and questions arose: Why was this happening now, when we had achieved our country's dream for independence? Why should our countries' merger cause others to be so angry? What harm was this merger doing to them? Was the bombing the work of Anti-Malaysia saboteurs or a mad bomber? What were they trying to achieve?

In many ways, when we didn't have television, the horror of an incident was not brought home to us so tangibly. But now the sight of moving images with all their sound and fury made it hard to escape the drama and pain of the people engaged in conflict. Technology was both a gift and a curse. One of the most terrible scenes to witness on television was the assassination of U.S. President John F. Kennedy on November 22 that year. Though he was not our leader, through films and now television, we had come to regard him as a charismatic, popular president. On the small screen, we saw the presidential motorcade come into view, with the president in an open-topped car, his wife beside him. Huge crowds thronged the streets of Dallas. President Kennedy was waving, his face beaming with a big smile, his forelock sweeping across his brow. Then, in the next moment, three shots rang out, and the president slumped sideways into his wife's lap. No one had registered what had taken place. The motorcade was still moving. Even Jackie Kennedy did not realise what had happened. She was nonplussed. Then, when realisation hit her, her face registered her anguish. Chaos reigned. And though we only saw it in black and white, we thought we *saw* the redness of his blood as it spattered on her face, hands, suit, and in her lap. The horror was indelibly etched in our minds. No one could have seen that scene and forgotten it. In May 1961, President Kennedy had vocalised his dream to Congress, of seeing the U.S.A. put a man on the moon. He would not see his dream fructify now.

Another horror lay in store for us – this time much closer to home.

The fifth bomb blast of the year occurred in December in Sennett Estate, the residential estate across Upper Serangoon Road directly opposite us in Kampong Potong Pasir. Someone threw the bomb across a rooftop. The bomb exploded. We all ran out of our houses when we heard the explosion.

"Sounds like war again," Pak Osman said.

The older folks knew what had caused the explosion but we youngsters did not. The loud noise was scary. Luckily the bomb had skidded off and exploded in the garden, so no one was hurt. Still, it was a manifestation of the unrest that had begun. Our dream to be an independent country was not without its dark side.

Of course we did not know that this was only the beginning of more strife.

Mak is skilled at using her Singer sewing machine, which accounts for my brothers and sisters dressed in outfits of the same fabric,1962. Phine is second from left.

Sisters in dresses with the same fabric design at a funfair, 1965.

A typical coffee-shop. Although this one was in Tanjong Rhu,
it is similar to the ones found in many kampongs like Potong Pasir.
(From the National Archives)

Dying To Be Free
(1964)

IT SHOULD BE lovely when a girl approaches her seventeenth year. She would be in the bloom of youth – standing on the threshold of womanhood. It should be. But it wasn't so for Parvathi. In many ways Parvathi's beauty was her downfall. Her father used it to lure suitors, and convinced them that he did not need to pay any of them a hefty dowry. It didn't matter to him if the suitor was fat or thin, or too old and ugly for his beautiful daughter. He was only concerned with getting rid of her.

Parvathi came to me weeping.

"What can I do? What can I do?" She moaned.

She was my best friend. Her whole life had been one of deprivation. The floor of her family hut was mud-packed, their possessions meagre. Parvathi had no education, no prospects in life except to marry well. We had a childhood pact – if our fathers forced us to marry, we would run away. We had sealed our agreement with our saliva, spitting a pearl-drop into each other's palms, then mixing and rubbing our palms together. Her father and mine had threatened us with this fate ever since we reached puberty. This Damocles sword hung over us. Women who were free to choose who they married would not understand the fear and horror that crippled us. I was four years younger than she was, so my father had not made any plans yet. But Parvathi's father had. He was always drunk and he had other wives and children, and came home to Parvathi's mother only when he desired her. Plus he needed money to feed his drinking habit, and was not opposed to being a pimp to his own daughter.

"This time my father is really serious. The man he has found is a widower with three young children. The man is marrying to provide a nursemaid for his kids! He is so old! Forty plus. He works as a butcher. Half his face had been damaged by some acid, so the skin is all scrunched up like wrinkled leather."

I tried to imagine being married to a man like that, and felt repulsed. Not just because of his looks but because we would have nothing in common. I'd rather die. But I did not say any of this to Parvathi. My heart contracted painfully for her.

"How I am dying to be free..."

"I'll run away with you," I said, though not very convincingly. I did not want to hurt my mother. But a pact had to honoured.

"No!" Parvathi said. "I won't let you. I'll set you free from our pact. You're educated. Your mother has sacrificed so much to put you through school. You need to finish school and do well to make her feel it has been worth it. This is not your battle. It's mine. I also want *you* to succeed — *for me*. It's vital for me to know that a kampong girl can make good and change her circumstances. Promise me!"

"I promise. I promise that I'll try my hardest to succeed, for you, for my mother, for myself. I will live my life in the best way possible, do the things you and my mother could not do..."

But she was not through.

"Promise me that you will live your life as a *free* person. You will fight against anyone who tries to oppress you. If you treasure freedom and live your life like that, *know* that you are making me happy wherever I may be..."

"Are you going to run away on your own then?"

"I'm thinking of it. But I don't know how my mother is going to survive if I go. All that I earned from the paper factory is given to her. She needs the money to buy the medicine for my brother. Yet I want to lead my own life too. But I'm good for nothing. How will I manage…?"

"You're not good for nothing," I said, far too strongly. "You're a clever, loving person. Good fortune is just not on your side. When I finish school and get a job, I will help you. I promise. Look, I've saved the money I got from selling the comics. You can have it all. Mak gave me a pair of gold earrings last year. You can pawn or sell them."

"Oh, Phine…" She said, her voice charged with emotion.

Then she reached out and hugged me, her long hair draping over my shoulders. She was taller than me so I felt small in her arms. We were twinned in despair. I was sad and angry at the same time. An uneducated kampong girl seemed so powerless. Parvathi's warm body shook with sobs. I too wept. I did not know then that it was going to be our last embrace.

"I wanna hold your hand, I wanna hold your hand," Karim sang.

He was our kampong boy who had made good. For years his musical talent lay hidden as he went about doing his smelly job of clearing the buckets from the village out-houses. But encouraged by fellow villagers and Pak Osman in particular, who recognised his gift, he found a gig that gave him his first opportunity. Then he ended up playing professionally in a band at the cabaret at *Great World* on Kim Seng Road.

Karim was singing a song by a new boy-band sensation called The Beatles, from Liverpool, England. On February 9, the four boys appeared on the *Ed Sullivan Show* and created pop-music history. We had a belated telecast on TV, which we saw at the village coffee-shop, which had installed the TV to attract more customers. Previously, when we didn't have electricity, we wouldn't have been able to watch TV, so we were so grateful that now we could.

The *kopitiam* or coffee shop with its cement floor was open on two sides, with white marble table-tops and brown mahogany legs. Each table had an enamel spittoon under it. Black and white posters of Chinese women posing provocatively in high necked cheongsams slit at the thigh adorned the wooden walls. Most of the customers were men who wore singlets. Several trishaw-riders sat on their haunches on the chairs in their drawstring shorts, exposing the sinewy muscles of their brown legs. It required a lot of strength and stamina to ferry two passengers in a trishaw, especially if the customers were overweight and the riders had to ride uphill. Trishaws were a familiar sight on our roads, as most people could not afford a taxi. In the coffee shop, hot drinks were served in solid china cups and saucers. Trishaw riders tended to pour their hot drink into the saucer to cool it before drinking it out of the saucer. The spittoons were usually used by them as they often cleared their throats and spat into them.

So when our parents caught us behaving in an uncouth way, they would say, "Stop behaving like a *trishaw rider*!"

Of course we could not enter the coffee-shop as we were non-paying customers, so we viewed the TV from afar. There was a cluster of children all trying to get a view of the TV screen. To me, the American impresario, Ed Sullivan, looked strange, with his jowly cheeks hanging down on each side of his face. He introduced the Beatles and the house went wild – teenage girls screamed as the boys with the pudding-basin haircuts came on.

"If only girls would scream like that for me when I came on stage," Karim said.

His dream would never come true. Later in the same month, the management of *Great World* gave notice that it was shutting down due to financial loss. *Great World* was one of the three *Worlds*, besides *Happy World* and *New World*; entertainment centres for the ordinary family where there were fun-fair type stalls, shopping, food and a cabaret. So its demise not only affected all its employees, which included Karim, but also ordinary folk looking for value-entertainment.

The job loss threw Karim into depression. He was a good looking, well-built young man and had always been cheerful.

"I can't go back to shovelling shit," he confessed to Pak Osman.

Perhaps his former job had been tolerable when he did not know any other type of life, but now that he had been exposed to a different life, the idea of taking up his old job was repugnant to him.

"Maybe you can find another band to play with at *Happy World*. Or be a *jaga* or something," Pak Osman suggested. "You don't have to go back to your old job."

The word *jaga* is Malay for *watch* and it can be both a verb and a noun. Pak Osman meant a security guard. Many of the local *jagas* were Sikh men, recognisable by the turbans on their heads. They usually positioned themselves in front of buildings, and slept at night on roped *charpoys* or cots outside the building they were guarding. The kind of work they did wasn't exactly inspiring for a talented musician.

"*Ya*, maybe," Karim said listlessly.

Despite the aggravation caused by the Anti-Malaysia saboteurs, there was still a sense of hope in our country. Whilst we were now part of a larger united nation, we also retained our own country's identity. The Tourist Promotion Board decided that we needed our own symbol as a marketing tool to promote tourism, a symbol that would come to be associated with only Singapore, just like Big Ben is always associated with England and the Statue of Liberty with the United States.

In the *Sejarah Melayu* or Malay Annals, there was a story of how Singapore came to be named *Singapura*, our country's name in Malay. Prior to that, our island had been called *Temasek*, which was just a small fishing village surrounded by huge forests and swamps, inhabited by the indigenous Malays. A prince from Indonesia, Sang Nila Utama, standing on a hill in his own country, saw the stretch of golden sand along our island's beaches in the distance and was attracted. He sailed across the sea with his courtiers. When they landed and explored the island, he encountered a large animal with a hairy mane.

"What is the name of this creature?" He asked his courtiers.

"A *singa*, my lord."

"This is such a propitious sighting. I shall name this island *Singa-Pura*, for I forecast that it will be a great city one day."

The words 'singa' and 'pura' meant 'lion' and 'city' respectively in Sanskrit, and they carry the same meaning in Malay.

So it seemed appropriate that when looking for a symbol for our island-state, the Tourism Board would hark back to this legend and feature the fabled lion. But the lion was not unique to Singapore, as some other nations had already used it on their national flags and even to market their beer. Then some bright spark suggested that since Singapore was surrounded by the sea, that too should somehow be expressed in Singapore's symbol. Thus the *Mer-Lion* was conceptualised, a fantastical creature with a lion's head and the tail of a fish. The word *mer* is derived from the French word for *sea*. Perhaps our bright spark loved the famous song, "*La Mer*", a song written in 1943 by French composer, lyricist and singer, Charles Trenet. It was a huge hit all over the world and for years after was still loved, even by non-French speaking people and was still featuring in the hit parade. In May, the sideways profile of the Merlion was launched with fanfare as the Tourism Board's logo.

"Half lion, half fish??" My father said with incredulity when the news broke on television. "The person who designed it must be on LSD! It won't work."

But he was wrong, wasn't he?

My father's friend, Ah Gu, who was Chinese-educated and had his ears to the ground on every aspect of Chinese education, was incensed when the police raided Nanyang University. Some of the students were suspected of being communist activists.

"A thousand policemen, I tell you," Ah Gu said with a raised voice. "They sent a thousand policemen to arrest fifty-one students! Why is it that people associate studying Chinese and having cultural ties with China as our link with communism?"

"Hush, Gu!" My father warned him. "These are sensitive times."

In that my father was correct.

Another bomb exploded, this time at RAF Changi. We appeared to be punished for joining Malaysia. *Konfrontasi*, the programme of aggression instigated by Indonesian President Sukarno, was designed to weaken the resolve of our nation.

In our kampong, we lived and worked together as one large, friendly community but at the same time we celebrated our ethnic diversity. Malay, Chinese, Peranakans, Indians and Eurasians lived next door to each other without rancour; our doors open to each other. But *konfrontasi*, anti-Malaysia campaigns, and the communists' agitations, all took their toll on racial harmony. Tension intensified from the previous year.

On July 21, many of our Malay villagers, including Pak Osman, Encik Salim and Karim got ready to celebrate Prophet Mohammed's birthday. They dressed up in their religious best, wearing a freshly pressed *baju* or tunic and sarong. On their heads, they wore a *songkok*. They were going to join a procession that was to run from *The Padang*, the lawn area in front of City Hall to Kampong Geylang Serai.

It was a huge event, as thousands of Muslim devotees turned up. We listened to the commentary on *Rediffusion* and felt somewhat connected, as so many of our villagers were there too.

The announcer said that they estimated that 25,000 Muslims had turned up for the event. There were opening prayers on the steps of City Hall, followed by speeches. We looked forward to the news on the evening's television telecast, which always began at 6PM, so we could witness the joyous celebrations.

What we did not expect to see was chaos and carnage.

Apparently, at 5PM, when the walking procession was near *Lorong 3*, Geylang, a group strayed away from the main procession. A policeman – it was rumoured that he was a Chinese policeman, which was a significant fact – tried to persuade the group to go back and join the main procession. Instead of complying, the group attacked the policeman, and that was how the riot started. Suddenly it was not about being disciplined. Instead, the issue became why a Chinese person should interfere with a Malay proceeding. The tension of the previous year had come to a head. Fights broke out amongst the Chinese onlookers and the twenty-five thousand Muslims.

Pak Osman and Encik Salim came home without Karim.

"Poor Karim, poor Karim. The whole thing was utter madness," Encik Salim said. "People were dying in order to be free to practise their religion and protect their culture – when they already have that freedom!"

"It's so tragic! How has it developed into a racial thing?" Pak Osman said.

Worse was yet to come.

Rediffusion announced, "Urgent! Urgent! We are bringing you important news. The government is imposing a curfew all around the country. Everyone has to stay indoors from 9PM to 6AM..."

Apparently a group of youths, not content with unleashing their wrath on the procession, armed themselves with *parangs* and *changkols* and they roamed the island, trying to injure and slaughter those in their path. It aroused terror in our hearts. The Federal Reserve Unit and the riot squad were brought in. A curfew was imposed all around the country. Twenty-three people were killed and nearly 500 were injured, Karim amongst them. He lay in hospital, his life hanging on a thread.

When he was eventually discharged from hospital, he was a shadow of the man he used to be. He had sustained severe injuries and could not walk. He had lost his sense of dignity when he was laid off from employment, but now he lost his most treasured possession – his capacity to sing.

Even the atmosphere in our village changed. Where the different races used to live harmoniously, there was now a growing suspicion of each other. It worsened in September. On the 3rd, in Geylang Serai, a Malay trishaw-rider was found murdered. The Malays believed that it was retaliation against the July Riots and that his attackers were ethnic Chinese. So another racial riot erupted around Geylang and the Peranakan enclaves of Joo Chiat and Siglap. But the violence was not confined to those areas- it spread all round the country so another country-wide curfew was imposed. Our village felt the impact of this particular riot more than the other one, as rioters ran into our village chasing each other, whilst some sought refuge. We shivered and crouched behind closed doors and shuttered windows as running footsteps went past. We heard shouts of agony as *parangs* were wielded. The memory of it stays lodged in my head, surfacing as incoherent nightmares. In this riot, 13 people were killed and 106 injured.

Malaysia's acting Prime Minister, Tun Abdul Razak, appealed for calm. He wanted people to understand that the fight was not between local Malays and Chinese. It was believed that Indonesian saboteurs, bent on creating instability in the newly formed Malaysia, had instigated and orchestrated the chaos.

"This fight is not between Malays and Chinese," Pak Osman reiterated Tun Razak's message. "We must bear this in mind and not be led astray by the saboteurs. We have lived in harmony before and we can live in harmony again."

But still it was not a year that could be forgotten.

Certainly not for me anyhow.

Just when the chaos in the country looked like it was settling down, a personal situation took a turn for the worse. Parvathi was betrothed. I was shocked that she was going to become a sacrificial lamb. But then it's always easy to make a judgement when one isn't caught up in the trauma. What choice had she got? She had no education, no money and little opportunity to overcome her circumstances.

When I got home from school, my mother handed me the earrings that I had given to Parvathi.

"She wants you to have these back," Mak said.

I shuffled nervously on my feet. Mak had taken so long to save the money to buy the hooped earrings for my special *Rabbit Year* birthday the previous Chinese New Year. She must be furious at me for giving them away.

"She ... she needed money ... and I thought she might be able to pawn them..."

My mother went quiet for a few moments.

"I have raised you right," she said, the stern look dissolving from her face. "Indeed, you should give away your prized possessions to help others in great need. But you should have told me. I could have found another way!"

Truly, my mother was a very special lady.

When Parvathi got home from work, I confronted her.

"Why are you giving up?" I asked her. "You can still live your life."

"I have no choice. I have no choice," she repeated in utter despair.

"Come," I said, trying to lift her spirits. "Let us go and sit under the angsana tree. I have brought another book to read to you."

It made me happy that she could enter a different world for an hour, and pretend that all was well. I will always remember that day. Her eyes were ringed with black kohl, her hands dyed in a pattern of henna, ready for her wedding. She looked beautiful as she leant against the trunk of the tree. She was not quite seventeen.

"Thank you, Phine. Remember what I said before, if you treasure freedom and are really living your life fully, *know* that you are making me happy wherever I may be." Then she concluded. "You know, now that I have made my decision, I am actually quite resigned and feel so calm."

Of course I had assumed that the decision she was referring to was the decision to marry the ugly old suitor that her father had found for her. But I assumed wrong.

The next morning when I heard her mother shrieking, I knew.

Pravathi had decided that dying was her only way to be free. She had swallowed all of the pills that were normally used to sedate her brother.

I could not bear to see her or to send her off to her cremation. I was told afterwards that she was placed in an open coffin, as was the Indian custom, bedecked with flowers. In the end, she still left our kampong like a bride. The morning of her funeral, I ran away into the grasslands that surrounded our village, wide fields of wild grass called *lallang*. The stiff, tall grass, some taller than a child's height, had razor-sharp edges and could nick your bare flesh drawing blood. I ran crazed through the tall lallang and allowed it to draw blood.

Pravathi's words went round and round in my head, *I have no choice. I have no choice.*

The Lion Must Learn
To Roar Again
(1965)

ON MY FOURTEENTH BIRTHDAY, on March 18, the first human took a walk in outer space. It is an amazing feeling when you realise that you are living through what is going to be such a great historical moment. Soviet cosmonaut Aleksei Leonov was one of the twenty Soviet Air Force pilots selected to be part of the first group of cosmonauts in 1960. Initially, he was supposed to take the walk on the Vostok 11 mission, but this was cancelled. In the end, the historic event occurred on the Voskhod 2 space flight instead. It was reported that *he was outside the spacecraft for 12 minutes and 9 seconds, connected to the craft by a 5.35 meter tether.*

That was the only uplifting news for the month.

I had no cause for celebration anyway, as my best friend, Parvathi, was gone. Every place I went, there were reminders of her. The loss did not seem to get easier with time, as people said it would. But sometimes when I was in our special place, I swear I could hear her laugh, and goose-pimples would appear on my arms. I wanted to believe that her other-worldly laughter was her way of letting me know she was all right. If I were a lion, I knew it was up to me to learn how to roar again.

Certainly for us in Singapore, it was a month beset with troubles like bomb explosions. The first happened on the 10th just before my birthday, at MacDonald House on Orchard Road. The creamy facade and building was designed by Palmer and Turner in neo-Georgian style and was built in 1949 for the Hongkong and Shanghai Bank, and was the first fully air-conditioned office building in South East Asia. MacDonald House contained the offices of British, American and Australian companies.

"At 3.07PM today, a bomb went off at Macdonald House, killing three people and injuring thirty-three others." The radio announcer's voice was sombre.

Many of our villagers were clustered around the radio.

"Ya Allah!" Pak Osman cried. "When is all this going to stop?"

"The trouble is," Ah Gu said. "President Sukarno has withdrawn his country from being a member of the United Nations, as it did not support his policy against Malaysia. So now he thinks he does not have to answer to the UN, and can intensify his terrorism."

"The man is crazy, " Encik Salim said. "Malaya and Singapore will never be part of Indonesia, no matter what terror he unleashes!"

Much later, it was learnt that the bomb at Macdonald House had been planted by two Indonesian saboteurs. Our whole country was on tenterhooks, not knowing where the next bomb was going to be planted. Movements were severely restricted and people felt nervous and distressed. Nowhere was safe. We lived under a huge cloud of darkness.

Almost immediately, the next bomb went off the following day at the National Library on Stamford Road. A few days later, another exploded at the Hock Lee Bus depot. Meyer Road in the Katong area stretched from Tanjong Rhu Road to Tanjong Katong Road. This time the saboteurs struck in that area, and the bomb blasted off part of the sea-wall, letting the tide in. The month ended with another explosion that hit the water mains at St. Francis Road. The burst pipes sent fountains of water spouting into the air. Another time, this might have been an occasion of merriment for kampong kids, as they would have leapt around and fooled about in the water spray, but this time it was serious – and potentially dangerous.

The year was peppered with bomb threats and hoaxes.

"No school today, no school today," students were told when we tried to attend school. This time the threats were closer to home, at St. Andrew's School, the missionary school across from our village, and in my own school, Cedar School. Luckily the bombs did not detonate.

"It would be easier if I just die in a bomb explosion," Karim moaned.

"Karim!" Pak Osman admonished him. "Don't say that. People care for you. You've always had a wonderful spirit. You used to whistle while you worked, even when the job was abhorrent, clearing all those smelly buckets from the outhouses. Everyone admired you."

"But I could walk then. And sing..."

"You can't walk because you're not trying. One's character is not tested in happy times, it is tested in adversity. I'm confident that you still have that amazing spirit in you. Come on, lean on me and you can start with a few steps..."

The older man reached out to help the younger man.

"Lean on me," Pak Osman said. "You can lean on me."

Politically, the new countries that together formed Malaysia were not leaning well on each other. Singapore's merger with

Malaya, Sabah and Sarawak seemed like a marriage of ill-matched partners, though the poor match did not manifest itself until the partners started living together. Like all new marriages, initially there was the excitement of a fresh, untested relationship where there was scope for sharing and discovering. For a while, these triumphed over the other's new ways and irritating habits. Malaya, Sabah and Sarawak had a large proportion of ethnic Malays, whilst Singapore had a larger percentage of ethnic Chinese. It was this imbalance that was a source of contention. Something our Prime Minister Lee Kuan Yew said at a speech to workers about a Malaysian Malaysia did not sit well with the Malays. His words were interpreted as trying to question the validity of the status of Malays and of eroding their position in the nation.

"*Aiiyah!*" Encik Salim said impatiently. "The governments are behaving like quibbling children! *I want more this and more that. You must do this and I will do that.* Nobody wants to give in."

"Indeed," Pak Osman said. "Each is clinging to what he wants. Why don't they focus on the bigger picture? No matter what race we are, we are all in the same nation!"

"Correct! Correct!" Ah Gu said. "If we only focus on external characteristics, we will always be different, Malays, Chinese, Indians and Eurasians. But inside we are all the same – we are all brothers-*what*!"

"Wow, Gu!" My father said. "So how come you're so *cheem* today?"

Cheem is the Teochew and Hokkien word for *deep*, which suggests a profound outlook. My father was having a humorous dig at his close friend. They always spent their evenings together with a pint of *Guinness*, discussing politics.

"That's the trouble with you," Ah Gu said to my father. "Just because I'm Chinese-educated and you are English-educated, you overlook my intelligence! Just because I can't express myself well in English does not mean I don't have deep thoughts, you know."

"Okay why don't we see if another pint of *Guinness* will bring up more of your deep thoughts then," my father laughed.

It was not an easy year for the PAP. Besides our troubles with the *Konfrontasi* terrorists, we continued to have trouble from the communist agitators. The communists had always appealed to susceptible minds, like school children and college students. The previous year, they had infiltrated Nanyang University, and the police had raided its premises and arrested those involved. Now the communists instigated demonstrations in various parts of the country and organised a large scale one for May Day on May 1 – a day set aside all over the world to celebrate the contribution of workers. Five thousand students gathered at Farrer Park. When the police told them to disperse, they started to pelt the police with stones, so the riot squad was called in to fire tear gas at them.

"The world has gone mad," Pak Osman, our village elder, said.

When a marriage breaks down, it is equally traumatic for both partners. No one goes into a marriage without dreams, hopes and the belief that it will last forever. People on the outside sometimes tend to over-simplify the couple's actions and say that the partner who initiated the divorce is intolerant or selfish. But this is only an outside view – and an external perception can be wrong because it does not have all the facts. There are so many factors that may have been considered, factors that will impact others disastrously if the turbulent marriage proceeds. Sometimes, it requires wisdom to know when a relationship is truly over, and sometimes it requires courage to say so. Limping along in a marriage that is painful or empty can have terrible repercussions for those forced to stay in it; the joylessness of such a marriage will drain the vitality of the spirit.

Malaysian Prime Minister, Tunku Abdul Rahman reluctantly admitted that he believed that the marriage between Malaysia and Singapore was over.

He said, *"This is the most painful and heartbreaking news I have to break."*

For a few months, there had been rumours circulating of this impending stalemate, but we were still shocked. Tunku Abdul Rahman had a genial face and he was very well respected in Singapore even before we joined Malaysia. He went on to say that the relationship between Malaysia and Singapore was no longer tenable.

"We have reached the stage where it is difficult to agree on anything at all, however trivial..."

He also said that he was concerned that if there was no break, there would be serious communal conflict.

The separation was final. It was August 9.

Although our Prime Minister, Mr Lee Kuan Yew, had held a press conference at 4.30PM, we didn't see the telecast till the evening, when *TV Singapura* commenced. A big crowd of villagers gathered around the television set in our village coffee-shop. Our prime minister came on air, his face looking wretched. He was sitting on a long bench with his other ministers, their white shirts stark on the black-and-white TV set. The young producer of the show, Chandra Mohan, had been instructed not to depict the Prime Minister in any state of heightened emotion. However, he was so stunned at the emotional distress exhibited by the Prime Minister that he defied production rules-he gestured to the cameraman to carry on filming. And that was how the iconic moment was captured with a close-up shot.

When Mr Lee came on, his face was already crumpled from the day's proceedings. His eyes were lacklustre, his mouth working wordlessly in inner agony. He started by saying, "*For me, it is a moment of anguish. You see the whole of my adult life, I...*" He could not go on. He bit his lower lip and sat back in his seat, his whole body language conveying utter distress. The other ministers bowed their heads. Still Mr Lee tried to continue, "*I ... I have believed in the merger and unity of the two territories. You know, they are people connected by geography, economics and ties of kinship...*" His voice stumbled over the word *ties* but he managed to finish the sentence. He stopped and bit his lip again. Then as if unsure of his own resolve, he said in a voice that was shaking with emotion, "*Would you mind if we stopped for a while?*"

When he took out his big white handkerchief to wipe his eyes, all of us watching cried with him, some softly, some bawling loudly. We were weeping for him, for our country, which had been rudely ousted from a nation we had believed in, and for our own precarious future.

"*Ya Allah!*" Pak Osman cried, "What will become of us now?"

"Mr Lee Kuan Yew said many times that *Singapore cannot survive on its own*," Ah Gu said. "But now it looks like we have to."

The death of one's dream is a painful thing. Perhaps Parvathi gave up because her dream had also died. Someone once said, "*When dreams die, life is like a winged bird that cannot fly.*" So long as one can dream, one can live in hope.

Lee Kuan Yew had been sworn in as Prime Minster at the young age of thirty-six in 1959. Now he had to bear the responsibility of being the father of Singapore at age forty-two. We had gone from being British to Singapore citizens, to Malaysian citizens, and now we were birthed again as Singaporeans. It was a forced birth, like a Caesarean, more traumatic than if it had been natural. The Malaysian flag was hastily taken down from all government buildings and the Singapore flag was raised in its place. Britain was one of the first countries to accept Singapore as an independent, sovereign nation. Other countries followed suit, expressing their regret but offering support, as Singapore requested to remain in the Commonwealth.

"*I'm not here to play somebody's games,*" Mr Lee Kuan Yew, now much more composed, said in his next telecast, "*I have a few million lives to account for. Singapore will survive!*"

His vigour and determination filled us with renewed hope. We were so proud of him. In fact, seeing his vulnerability had made us realize that he was a human being who was trying to work for the greater good. And you have to respect a man for that, no matter what your political leanings might be.

"Karim," my mother said, taking his guitar to him. "I am still having trouble with the chords of *Bengawan Solo*. Can you help me?"

Anneke Grönloh, a female Dutch singer, had sung the Indonesian song about the Solo River in Central Java. It was written by Gesang Martohartono in 1940 and was such a popular song during the second world war that even the Japanese loved it, taking it back to Japan and translating it into their language. It was sung in Keronchong style, which Peranakans absolutely adored, so we made it one of our traditional songs. The previous year, Anneke had won the Eurovision contest with a Dutch song, so some of the songs she had sung in Bahasa Indonesia had also been revived locally and were played on the radio. Her other popular song, especially loved by children, was *Burong Kakak Tua*.

Karim and my mother had sung and played music together at many of our evening soirees which Karim had initiated. But since the riot of July last year, when he had sustained his injuries, he had withdrawn into himself. Fortunately Pak Osman had encouraged the young man to try to walk again, and Karim could now hobble about on a *tongkat*, the Malay word for a *walking stick*. But he had not played a guitar for months, as the injury to his throat had affected his vocal chords and prevented him from singing, which he so loved. In his frustration, he had given the guitar to my mother.

"No, I can't, *Nonya*," he demurred.

"*Bengawan Solo, riwayat mu ini,*/ Begawan Solo, your legend is this..." My mother sang the song anyway, twanging the strings in odd places as if she was all thumbs.

"Eh Nonya!" Karim said. "Spare my ears! You must be out of practice!"

"I am out of inspiration," Mak said, smiling. "I need your help."

She handed his guitar back to him. He caressed the guitar fondly.

"All right, all right!" Karim said, not at all deceived either by my mother's or Pak Osman's wiles. "You all win. I will try. The lion must learn to roar again."

In December, television sets were assembled locally and marketed under the brand name *Setron*. This made a TV set more affordable for ordinary folks and for people like us in the villages. My father, Ah Tetia, always received a bonus close to Christmas, as he worked for an English company. We loved that time of year! He was like the English Santa Claus, bringing home presents and food we normally could not afford to buy. The previous year, he had brought home a packet of English fish-and-chips, wrapped in newsprint, bought from the best chippy in Serangoon Gardens, one of the strongholds of the British army. This time, to our family's surprise, he came home with a TV set! He was assisted by his weight-lifting mates, Rajah and Salleh.

"*Gila* or what? Have you gone *mad*? Have you spent our month's money for food on this thing?" My mother said, pretending to be cross.

But we could tell from her tone that she was as excited as we were. Our own television set! How far we had come! First electricity and now this. Maybe one day we might even be able to install a tap in our house and we could have running water.

There was only one small table in our house, pressed against the wall opposite our beds. So my father set the TV onto the table. We buzzed about the men as they set the TV up.

"We want to watch the SEAP Games telecast," my father said, justifying his purchase. "Tan Howe Liang is still participating and pushing for gold again."

There wasn't going to be an actual telecast of the games but just highlights, but my father twisted the truth to suit himself. SEAP stood for Southeast Asian Peninsular Games, which were to be held in Malaysia later in the month. Tan Howe Liang was still Singapore's contender for the Lightweight division in weight-lifting. My father, Rajah and Salleh spent weekends lifting weights in our sandy backyard, so they had been following Tan Howe Liang's career closely.

That evening, all our immediate neighbours came to sit on the floor of our house to watch TV with us. People brought *apok-apok* – Malay curry puffs and other snacks – to share, turning the space between our beds and the wall into a cinema auditorium. My siblings and I sat on the beds. I wished Parvathi was with us to share this special moment. But she was not. I wondered when I would stop thinking about her or stop wishing I could feel her presence.

The telecast began at 6PM and the news carried the headlines about our *Yang di Pertuan Negara*, Encik Yusof Ishak's inauguration, as our country's first president. This was followed by *Sea Hunt*, an

American scuba-diving, underwater drama series which starred Lloyd Bridges.

Later in the month, my father and his mates, Rajah and Salleh, did watch the highlights of the SEAP Games. They leapt from the floor when they heard that Tan Howe Liang had won his gold medal. This was the man who would go down in Singapore sports history later as winning the first medal in the Olympics, even if it was silver. Though a bad year in Singapore politics, it was a good year in sporting achievements. In all, Singapore won 26 gold, 23 silver and 27 bronze medals. It was such a boost for the ailing spirit of our country. The icing on the cake was the amazing win by an eleven-year-old girl, Patricia Chan, in her swimming events. She won eight gold medals!

"See! See!" My father said triumphantly. "Nobody can keep Singapore down forever."

"*Ya, ya!*" Everyone watching the telecast agreed.

Our gallant sportsmen showed that Singapore could succeed. They had the tenacity of young lions and reflected the new spirit that was beginning to take a foothold in our new nation. As Premier Lee Kuan Yew had said, Singapore *will* survive. Of course, it would require a strong government and astute handling of the situation to propel Singapore out of Third World Status. The people had to give the government a free hand to make changes and everyone had to work extremely hard.

Most certainly with our lack of natural resources, it would be an uphill task. Nonetheless, we felt confident that we would find our own identity, discover our own strengths.

Indeed, the lion must learn to roar.

About the Author

JOSEPHINE CHIA, is a Peranakan who is proud of her heritage. She was born and raised in Kampong Potong Pasir in the 1950s.

Since then, she has picked up BA Honours from the University of Singapore and an MA in Creative Writing from Bath Spa University College, United Kingdom.

Her short stories were first published in *SINGA*, the literary Journal of Singapore and also in *The Straits Times*. After moving to England in 1985, Josephine won the Ian. St. James Award and other prizes for both her short stories and articles; some of were published in various anthologies. She also received a highly commended prize from the Society of Women Writers & Journalists for her travel article.

An eclectic writer. Her fiction oeuvre includes two novels and a collection of short stories, while her non-fiction collection consists of a cook book and two others on yoga.

Josephine was a council member of UK's Society of Women Writers & Journalists until she returned back to Singapore in May 2012. She taught creative writing, yoga and cookery in the UK.

Josephine currently runs creative writing workshops for the National Book Development Council Singapore, the National Library Board and is facilitator for Ministry of Education's Creative Arts Program (CAP). She was also featured in NBDCS's Youth's Literary Festival and National Arts Council's Words Go Round program for schools and in the Singapore Writers Festival.

For more information on Josephine, visit her website:
www.josephinechia.com

Also by Josephine Chia

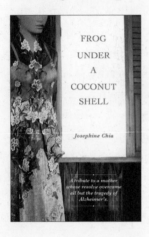

Frog Under A Coconut Shell
ISBN: 978-981-4276-84-9

Frog Under A Coconut Shell translates in Malay as 'kakak bawah tempurong', an idiom which likens someone to a frog that lives under a coconut shell, believing the shell to be its entire world.

It is a reference to both the author's mother and the author herself. The author's mother, although herself uneducated and living a parochial existence in a small village, believed and and fought hard to realise a greater vision – the right to educate her daughter. And the author had ot deal with the challenges of crossing boundaries both geographical and emotional. This moving tale weaves the lives of both women together, beautifully evoking the experience of living in 1960s Singapore, and painting in heartwarming detail, a Peranakan's woman's journey from the bloom of her youth to her later affliction with Alzheimer's.